PUDL⋯N YOUR⋯ATH

ARLYN VIERKANT; SUSAN SCHROEDER
VIERKANT

PublishAmerica
Baltimore

First printing

PublishAmerica has allowed this work to remain exactly as the author intended, verbatim, without editorial input.

Softcover 9781627729734
PUBLISHED BY PUBLISHAMERICA, LLLP
www.publishamerica.com
Baltimore

Printed in the United States of America

DEDICATION

This book is dedicated to the reader, the man or woman who is able to recognize the humor that can be found in most of our human interactions. These are the folks who do an honest day's work, take responsibility for their families, worship a Living God, show kindness to others, and still have a few minutes every once in a while to chuckle at the bumbling behaviors that surround them.

FOREWORD

In the observation and analysis of human behavior, it is extremely tempting to pontificate, to over-evaluate, and to develop constructs that have the fragility of a plastic sheet covering the cargo on the back of a pickup speeding down the highway in a driving rain storm.

The players on the stage of life are judged by their observable behaviors while their actual motivations remain hidden from the prying eyes of the self-appointed and often highly biased critic.

The observer is a captive of his own culture, socioeconomic status, socialization, life experience, and even of his possible indigestion at the time that the "happening" plays out in front of his eyes. I have traveled this road in several of the books that I have authored and have been occasionally "roasted" by my editors and readers who have urged me to "lighten up" and to "smell the roses." Unlike former efforts, this book will be presented in "incident" form rather than in chapters. It is felt that this will contribute to the undisciplined flow of thought that reflects the author's penchant to follow the rabbit, regardless of the trail which the rabbit chooses to hop.

I am convinced that the ridiculous, the mind-boggling, and even the "profane" are constantly enacted all around us and are "learning moments" given to us if we will merely be aware of the circus of life that is being performed as we take our walk through this temporal stage of life.

As the old police drama used to intone, "The incidents are real, only the names have been changed to protect the 'not so' innocent."

ACKNOWLEDGEMENTS

In all of my books, I have relied very heavily upon the editing expertise and the "take no prisoner" criticism of my daughter, Silvana. In addition to her full-time employment and rich lifestyle, she has expended innumerable hours "cleaning up" my grammar and placing a brake on my natural inclination for wordiness. She has even reserved some time to laugh with me as we shared common experiences.

A big expression of appreciation also has to be extended to all those who have so willingly stumbled into my awareness, usually never appreciating the laughs that they have provided or knowing that they would someday be recorded as "examples" in a chuckling old man's book.

This is the first work that I have co-authored with my wife, Susan. It seemed only fit and proper to do so as she has often been forced to sit by and listen to tales of the unusual over and again. She may also have been a "player" in some of the episodes.

PUDDLE 1

WHEN WORD MEANINGS ARE NOT OBVIOUS

A young married student e-mailed me late one evening just a few hours before class to inform me that she would not be in attendance for the scheduled test. Her exact words, "I am very sorry that I cannot be in class tonight as I had to go home with the crud."

I promptly returned an inquiry to her statement, "Are you making reference to your husband or to some sort of physical ailment?"

Words have meanings.

PUDDLE 2

DRAMATURLOGICAL WIVES

It is interesting to observe the theatrics of mature married women when they are aware that peers of the same cohort are observing them. I dropped my wife off at a local parking lot so that she might commute with five other ladies to a distant workshop. The travelers were eying each other as bags were loaded into the vehicle of the designated driver. Suddenly my wife turned, gave me a big hug, and planted a big wet kiss on my mouth. This was in front of Ronald MacDonald and a cast of dozens munching French fries and hamburgers as they walked to their cars.

I was taken aback briefly as my wife is hardly the overtly demonstrative type of woman. Certainly, we had six children, but that is another issue for some other time.

Then I began to recognize a pattern based upon my observation of another unsuspecting husband walking unawares toward his wife with a large cup of coffee in his hand. Suddenly his wife pounced, grabbed him by an arm, whirled him into a vulnerable position, and applied a loudly smeared-patch of lipstick somewhere in the vicinity of his lower face. The poor victim almost lost his balance, most of his coffee, and gave the appearance of a rabbit who suddenly found itself looking up the muzzle of a twelve gauge shotgun. His eyes nervously met mine and then he slowly shrugged, pivoted, and went back for a java refill. Fortunately, we were the only two husbands seeing our wives off or the one-upmanship might have gotten out of hand.

What did this all mean? Was the kiss a cooler substitute for a marital branding iron? Do married women have to impress each other that the conjugal union remains intact? Is it possible that the "act" was a message to all other married women, "Hands off, he may not be much, but he is mine"? Was it possibly a statement of personal sexual orientation to all of the watching women that even though they might be living in close proximity for the next few days, there would be no option for "fun and games"? Could it possibly be symptomatic of salt deficiency?

While the overriding questions could not be answered, it all ended well. The women drove out of the parking lot with self-satisfied expressions. My gender mate exited the restaurant cautiously with his new cup of coffee, carefully surveyed his surroundings for the possibility of another ambush, and then imbibed with a contented sound of relief. I, in turn, drove home thinking, "Another interesting observation in life."

PUDDLE 3

WHO CONTROLS THE VERBAL HILL?

It is an observational connoisseur's delight to sit unobserved and to listen to two dominant, controlling individuals refusing to share the "microphone" in an attempted conversation. Mind you now, this was not an actual argument, but a struggle for dominance. On this particular occasion, it was between two self-focused individuals, male and female, who began a civil conversation, but soon became engaged in a "clash of the titans." Neither was the least bit interested in what the other was saying. I am sure that the topic which initially brought them together had long been lost in the struggle for dominance. In addition to the usual interruptions and the aggressive verbal insertions, the volume of each steadily escalated. The male's tone became increasingly harsh while the female's tone took on an unattractively whiny pitch. The male then adopted an unexpected tactic. He reverted to recounting stories from his youth, none of which were of the slightest interest to his adversary. Her frustrated tone escalated as he completed each anecdote with a loud "horse" laugh.

She, perhaps recognizing defeat, sought geographic advantage by getting up and walking out of her office into the hallway, while he slouched by her desk. Realizing that this was not working, she reached for her purse and took out her keys as if to signal that she was departing. The male then reluctantly stood up, walked into the hallway, and became distracted by another potential verbal sparring partner. The defeated lady returned to her office and quickly closed her door.

It was amusing to the observer, of course, but was it funny to the participants? Probably not at all. Why didn't she just say, "Look jerk, you are boring me"? Why didn't he proclaim, "Listen woman, I am Mr. Wonderful and I have a lot to say"? Well, they were both too nice, or were they? I am certain that some sort of toned-down communication could have brought the conversation to a quick end such as one of them saying, "I like listening to you, but I have to warn you that I am contagious with the Westmelian Plague."

PUDDLE 4

AN INVOLUNTARY VIEW FROM THE BALCONY

There is always a favorite incident and the following is mine. It will, in fact, probably be retold among my friends again and again for years to come. It was included in a previous book, *How High Does the Eyebrow Arch,* so if the reader thinks it is familiar, it probably is.

It started out on a nice summer day. My wife was out of state and everything was quiet and comfortable. Remembering her strict orders to water the plants on the back balcony at least once every other day, I decided to get the task accomplished before I would forget and, as a consequence, have before me an upset spouse glaring at some shriveled shrubbery upon her return. I filled two large jugs with water and made my way carefully across the living room to the sliding glass door leading out onto the balcony of our second floor apartment. I exited through the door and, being always mindful to conserve energy, slid it shut behind me. I carefully watered the thirsty plants and then turned to refill the containers for another trip. It was then that I realized that when one closes a sliding glass door with a security rod installed, it is important to make certain that it is latched up or else the rod will fall and secure the door from the inside. The design and installation were perfect. I was locked out. Being a veteran of the unexpected, after all we did raise six children, I immediately panicked. I looked out over the grounds for someone to assist me and spotted a comely young lady wearing a diminutive bikini sitting by the pool soaking up the sun. I opened my mouth to appeal for her help, but the words would not come out. What would her reaction be, along with that of possible observers, to an old codger yelling across the tree tops to this young lady with a message that would be something like, "Uh, little girl, how about coming up to my apartment and helping me get back in from my balcony?" No it didn't ring right. I could see the police arriving to question my motives and the next morning reading about how apartment dwellers should use caution about voyeurs attempting to lure young ladies into their apartments by pretending to be locked out on their balconies.

Now a man, experienced in meeting the challenges of the world, always has a fall-back plan. Mine was to throw myself over the balcony railing to the cement one-story below, roll to dissipate the energy generated by the force of the fall, and then walk around to the front of the building to enter the front door. Just as I was trying to decide whether to go head first or feet first, I heard a strange scratching sound from somewhere down below. Leaning as far out over the railing as I could and peering down into the patio area of the apartment below, I observed an elderly gentleman working on his patio with a rake. There was good and bad in this discovery. The good was that here was someone to whom I could appeal for help and possibly not get arrested for attempted bikini seduction. The bad news was that the unaware gardener was wearing nary a stitch of adornment. I sat down on the cement floor of the balcony to consider my dilemma.

Should I just wait for my wife to return? She would be gone only a few more days. I could survive drinking the mud-soaked water from the plants and nibble on the leaves from the overhanging trees. Then, an even more troubling thought hit me. Was the deadbolt on the front door thrown? If so, even if I found help, no one could get to me.

It was decision time. I leaned over and in the calmest voice that I could muster, I said, "Sir." The startled nudist peered up, tried to cover himself with his rake, and seemed frozen in space. I quickly explained my situation and asked him if he would kindly help me out by coming up to my apartment and opening the sliding glass door. If the deadbolt was set, would he contact management to see if they would come over with a ladder? The man disappeared and, a few minutes later, reappeared wearing a pair of walking shorts. The view was much improved. The potential for my rescue was much better. With a sheepish look on his his face, he nodded his willingness to assist me. It struck me that I had been so distracted in my first verbal contact, that I had not even noticed his face. Minutes later, I heard the glass doors open and the gentleman exited without allowing me to give him a thank-you hug. He lived there, below our apartment, for several months longer before moving on. I never saw any part of him again, but neither did I ever peer over the balcony again to look for him. Unasked question segment: Yes, I did have clothes on when I went out on the balcony, and no, I have never had a desire to rake any patio in the buff.

PUDDLE 5

CLEAR EYES

My wife is a pretty solid person in her thinking and in her assumption of personal responsibility. This, of course, is confirmed by the fact that she married me. When the children were small, she left the teaching profession and developed a small retail health food store so that she could be at home with the pre-school children during the day and still add some much needed income for our family.

She baked fresh bread and sold the usual line of herbs, vitamins, and food products, but, as reflected in her personality, she more importantly developed lasting social relationships with the customers which continued in later years when she returned to teaching.

One evening, upon returning to the store from my workplace, she met me with the question, "Did you know that everyone naturally has blue eyes?" Well, that ignorant I was not. "What in the world are you talking about," was my questioning response? She started laughing and told me about a visit that she had from a traveling Iridologist who had stopped by the store in an attempt to convince her to stock a certain "Colon Cleansing Product." The saleslady had stared into my wife's brown eyes and declared, "You really need to use this product yourself.

If you use it faithfully as directed, your entire system will be cleansed." My wife, being a little cynical and having a well-developed sense of humor, inquired as to how a customer would know that the product was successful in its intended objective? The Iridologist was shameless in her answer, "You can just look in a mirror and when your eyes return to their natural blue color, your system will have been cleansed." From that point on, whenever I am talking to an unfortunate brown-eyed person, I am always thinking, "Impaction!" If our paths ever cross and you notice me gazing deeply into your dark brown eyes, just remember, I may share your discomfort, but not your eye color.

PUDDLE 6

THE LITTLE TICKER

My wife is a terror to wrist watches. With any luck at all, most only last about a year. They just stop ticking. It is not the battery, it has something to do with her magnetism, or at least that is what we would like for her to believe. Well, one evening, we were making our annual trip to purchase another cheap watch from the local super center. She sorted through the menagerie of Chinese specials in time-keeping instruments. She is very particular. The device has to have a large dial, but still be feminine. It has to have a white face as, in her opinion, that color is less reflective of the fluorescent lights in her classroom. It has to have a gold tone case so it doesn't appear as cheap as it really is. And, finally, it has to have a strong wristband as she will no doubt snag it over and over again on table corners and other protrusions during the academic year. No colored beads are allowed on the case as such are too reminiscent of the eye-glass frames little girls wore when she was in grade school.

Well, during this hunt and search process, the clerk giggles, whispers, and hugs on a fellow employee who apparently is going off shift. Finally my wife makes a decision. She points to a watch in the case and asks to examine it.

Reluctantly, the clerk breaks off her conversation, opens the counter, and hands over the watch. After careful examination, such as most people would do with a Rolex, my wife announces,

"I will take this one." This is just the start of the story. As the clerk backed away following this momentous decision, she accidentally dropped the watch on the floor. She goes to one knee behind the counter to retrieve the "little ticker" only to look up to see my wife sprawled halfway over the counter looking down at her. Probably as much a startle response as it was defensive behavior, the clerk snarls, "What are you looking at?" My wife, being the gentle lady that she can occasionally be, merely responded that she had seen the watch hit the floor and wanted a different one that had not been dropped. The clerk quickly grabbed a box with a different watch of the same model and disappeared behind the cash register with both instruments. My wife can be relentless in such cases, well-schooled in how to get six children to eat their oatmeal. She can, in fact, be a "royal pain" when the right mood strikes. As the sacked product was handed over, she could not refrain from asking the loaded question, "Now this is not the watch that you dropped, is it?" In such circumstances, two men would have grinned at each other, slapped each other on the backside, and wished each other a good evening. Keep in mind that this was a transaction between two women. The clerk responded in anger which made my wife suspicious that she had packaged the abused watch. The result was a cancelled sale. A manager was involved but he, being male, merely listened, nodded, and apologized for the inconvenience. My wife returned to the store the next day and after making certain that the same clerk was not on duty, purchased another time piece. It was probably the same one that was dropped the night before, but shucks, we will be purchasing a replacement within a year anyway.

When such isolated unpleasant situations take place, keep in mind that there may have been other factors involved. Perhaps the clerk was attracted to her fellow employee who was going home from work and my wife had crashed a "window of opportunity." Could it have been something called PMS? Maybe the clerk was resentful that my wife had enough money to purchase such an exotic timepiece. Was there something going on that a psychoanalyst would classify as "transference"? Was the clerk upset at herself for being clumsy and dropping the watch? Who knows what was going on in the mind of each participant? In the fuss and furry of the moment, mere mortals relish the heat of the altercation and the battle of wills, especially if they are two women.

PUDDLE 7

MY FAVORITE OPPOSITE SEX

Have you ever noticed that men and women are different? I am certain that men are aware of such differences, but women oftentimes seem to be more heedless of such variations. For example, most men choose not to wear dresses or other articles of women's clothing. Women, however, choose to dress more like men. In today's society, in fact, I am not certain which male clothing pieces women *do not* wear. But where the largest discrepancy between men and women falls is in the arena of actions and behaviors.

Have you ever noticed that in the checkout line of any grocery store that the male shopper will have his credit card, checkbook, or cash ready by the time the clerk finishes scanning his purchases? In contrast, the typical female shopper will watch every scan for accuracy and then will wait until the purchases are loaded in her cart. The next step will be a slow and methodical unsnapping of her purse, the removal of a wallet or checkbook, a double checking of the bill, and then a slow consummation of the transaction. If a check is involved, it has to be made out in painful detail with the amount being carefully recorded in the transaction log. If photo identification is required, the entire process is repeated. Occasionally, the female shopper, upon showing her driver's license, will make excuses to the clerk about the photo, claiming that it was taken on a "bad hair day."

Then a "cutesy" conversation follows between the two women while the frustrated men waiting in line paw impatiently in their imaginary rodeo chutes.

In the same manner, watch a woman make her selections in the grocery aisles of the store. She will park her buggy on the right side of the aisle, block the left side with her body, and slowly read the contents of a can of "stuff" that she has routinely purchased over the past twenty years. Occasionally, depending upon her attitude, the woman will park her buggy perpendicularly to the shelves to ensure that other shoppers cannot pass through without a struggle. If a male reaches out to gently move the offending buggy, the female shopper will likely react as if Genghis Kahn had appeared in her bathtub.

My wife has a little trick that has never been tested but which would be exciting to observe in action. She has a little steel link chain, one end of which she clips to the frame of the shopping buggy and the other end to the strap of her purse which she leaves in the bottom of her cart. I have fabulous fantasies of a panicked purse snatcher grabbing her purse, running wildly through the store with the attached buggy on his heels, and my wife digging in her spikes while holding on to the rear of the cart. Such a scene would be worth losing a purse over.

There are some feminine behaviors that do frustrate me to the point that it is difficult to see humor therein. One is observing self-involvement to the point that they do not appear to care about the store or other customers. I have seen women walk down aisles eating produce that has not been weighed or checked out. I have seen one woman picking up one of those cheese dip and cracker packages, opening it for her kid to eat, and then discarding the wrapper on the floor before checkout. I have observed women peeling bananas and feeding them to their children while shopping. Oh yes, the peel is laid daintily on a nearby shelf. What is the store to do, weigh and reweigh each child upon entry and exit? I have seen mothers turn their children loose in toy departments to pillage and destroy while they complete their shopping rounds in other parts of the store. Upon return to the toy area, they will merely kick the mangled boxes to the side of the aisle and continue on.

The typical male of the species will usually bend over, pick up the product that some little urchin has thrown on the floor, and will replace it on the shelf. A man will order his little monster to remain in the cart seat, properly strapped in, or to stay by his side rather than to allow him to roam all over the store. Is it possible that men are more aware of cost "pass-through" or are they just neater by nature?

Then there is the "return process" that seems to be a fantasy land for many women. My wife has no compunctions about returning items to a store. I have seen her return a sack of peeled potatoes that had black spots on them. A watermelon that was white inside was plopped on the return counter. If a bottle does not have an inner seal properly affixed, back it goes. A while back she purchased a garbage disposal tool and, after using an axe to remove it from its secure wrapper, returned it without hesitation when she found it to be the wrong size. In the return section of the store, one will see items that have been ridden, bent, abused, and partially consumed. Does a man behave in such a manner? No, the man will eat the white watermelon, cut out the spots in the potatoes, and trust fate in regard to the missing inner seal in the creamer bottle.

PUDDLE 8

SOMEONE'S LISTENING

I was sitting in the main dining room of a nursing home with my mother one evening when a pompous, pseudo-adult male entered to visit a resident. This fellow had hair down to the small of his back, carefully secured by a rubber band, with an unusually small cap, bill reversed, perched on top of his head. He was obviously full of himself as he smirked his way through the congregated residents awaiting their evening meals. I turned to my mother and opined, "If that were my son, I would have to take him behind the barn and shoot him." I then noticed that another resident (an elderly lady) at a nearby table had been carefully eavesdropping on my conversation. I did not feel too much concern for my facetious, yet inappropriate, comment. This listener was suffering from moderate dementia and hopefully did not understand anything I had just said.

Approximately a week later, I was sitting in the same place at the same time. Again, the unusual specimen of humanity walked in. Without giving it much thought, I glanced over at the lady at the neighboring table. She grinned at me and said, "Bang-Bang."

PUDDLE 9

CHURCH ABLAZE

I was visiting a large, urban Presbyterian Church one pleasant Sunday forenoon while attending college. Several windows around the pulpit area had been opened to take advantage of the morning breeze. The service began in a predictable manner. However, what was unusual in this setting were the two large candelabra on either side of the pulpit. Presbyterians are usually not into candles as much as say, Lutherans, Roman Catholics, or even Methodists. It is probably a Calvinistic parsimony thing. Anyway, the wind gradually picked up outside. The candle flames were visibly invigorated by the increased oxygen feeding them and the pastor, obviously distracted, motioned for an usher to get the potential conflagration under control. The poor fellow obviously was not a fireman or even someone who had played with matches as a child. He certainly was not prepared for this "emergency." He first attempted to fan the flames out with his hands. Being unsuccessful, he moved on to a "birthday boy" approach, probably making a big wish that this assignment would just go away, and then started an intense blowing process. It was readily apparent that his wish would not be granted.

The pastor, by this time, had not only lost his train of thought, but his engine had long left the station. The congregation, in the meantime, was beside itself in attempting to suppress giggles which would accelerate into dangerous laughter, if not kept under control. There was a lot of choking sounds, eyes were averted, and I am certain that prayers for self-control were offered up. The preacher left the pulpit with a look of disgust on his face mixed with sarcastic amusement, picked up a candle snuffer leaning against the wall, and methodically extinguished all of the little flamers.

Many years later, do I remember the name of the church, of the name of the pastor, or the content of his sermon? Absolutely not, but I do vividly recall the little bald-headed man with the crimson face who unwillingly gained fame for life in a church full of Presbyterians on one Sunday morning.

PUDDLE 10

A SISTER WHO HAPPENED TO BE BLOND

My parents were farmers in the upper Midwest, known for its less than tropical winters, especially experienced by those who were raised in uninsulated farm houses, warmed by space heaters on the lower floor and by what little warm air drifted up through the stove pipe holes to the second floor. It was not unusual to turn back the sheets on a cold night and hear them "crack" from the cold air.

I was "blessed" with having a young sister, who happened to be blond. I wouldn't claim that she was a poster child for the blond jokes of later years, but she was a moving target for an older brother. One cold January night I planted an alarm clock in her bedroom set to go off at 2:30 in the morning. It was a masterful scheme. To hear the alarm jangle loudly, to hear two warm feet hitting the cold vinyl floor, and the expressed thought, "Oh, No!" was a reward to be treasured in years of memory. The next night, however, she was well prepared. She listened carefully for the giveaway ticking of the old alarm clock, located it, and pushed in the alarm button. She then settled in under the heavy quilts to enjoy some warmth and rest. Little did she know that the clock was merely a decoy. I had rigged an electric alarm up under some furniture, carefully disguising the electric cord from view. At 2:30 am, the loud electric alarm went off and continued while she desperately moved furniture and blankets in the frozen air to finally locate the mechanical antagonist.

I knew that revenge would be swift, but fortunately, our father, who valued his sleep at night, strongly informed us that there would be no more pranks of the clock variety played. Do blonds always lose? Not necessarily, but this one did. She didn't dare retaliate after dad's firm directive.

PUDDLE 11

COLD PIZZA

Pizza lovers and folks with exhibitionistic religious needs create a people watcher's paradise. Add extra sauce and blend in an empty-shell marriage and you really have something special.

One evening my wife and I were indulging at a local bistro when in walked a middle-aged couple. They immediately drew our attention by their obvious lack of affect and bodily hints at hemorrhoids. Each held under his/her left arm a large book of obvious library origin.

With great rigidity, they sat down at a table facing each other, wiped the top with a napkin to remove possible tomato sauce residue, and began to read.

No eye contact, no shared smiles, no evident interest in their immediate environment, not a word exchanged.

The waitress cautiously recorded the husband's food order, receiving no overt recognition of her presence, as his eyes never left his book. The order arrived in the usual 20 minute time frame and the patrons were courteous enough to lift up their books to allow the pizza pan to be placed on the table. At this point, both books were placed open on the table and the male began to raise up to God an extensive and long-winded table prayer...at least I hope that the message was directed to God, as fellow patrons were dragged unwillingly into the pretentious exercise. Finally, after a time frame which would have allowed another pizza to be processed and having never acknowledged each other's presence, the ritual was concluded. At this time, each picked up the book of choice in the left hand and probed for a slice of pizza with the right. Unfortunately, we had to leave at this point, allowing several questions to float along with the wonderful aroma of the eatery. At the consummation of this marriage, what was each passionately reading? Does either ever check to see if the other is still breathing? Do they ever suffer from hand confusion and take a misdirected bite out of a book? Was she really listening while he prayed? Was God listening or was He busy with the "Book of Life"? For readers of mechanical inclination, how did they turn a page in the book with both hands occupied? What was the disposition of spilled pizza sauce? Was the process intellectually stimulating or interpersonally avoidant? When did they cease to love each other? Did they ever love each other or was it the result of a shared library card? Why didn't they merely order pizza in?

Certainly there is sadness in this observation. Happiness can only be found in the fertile imagination of the observer.

PUDDLE 12

THE TRUTH ABOUT SANTA

A college instructor can become very excited, in fact ecstatic, when a student turns in a paper which is not only conforming to the assignment, but also interesting. While making notes for this book, I had given students an assignment to write an essay on the topic, "The most traumatic experience that has confronted you, how did you handle it, and what impact did it make on your life?" Simple enough of an assignment, but the return was somewhat discouraging except for one paper which was entitled, "The Truth About Santa." I received permission from the student to include the paper in this book, guaranteeing anonymity, and, of course, no compensation for the content. I have deleted certain comments which might lead to identification of the young person, but I include it below primarily in its entirety:

"I had grown up a sweet and caring person. I was also a devout Christian. I was so blindly faithful in the Lord and so trusting in my mother that I believed with every fiber of my being in God and Jesus, Heaven and Hell, and in Santa Claus. What my mother revealed to me at age eleven completely destroyed the foundation on which I had built my entire existence and caused me to lose my faith in God.

I was a fearful and neurotic child who found comfort in God. Knowing the consequences for falling short of God's expectations, I was constantly trying to please Him. I believed in Santa the same way that I believed in God. After all, my mother had told me that it was true. I could not be reasoned with but after being picked on constantly by my cohorts for my belief in Santa, I must admit that I started to have doubts. The first time I questioned my mother about the matter she lied and because I still believed her, I went back to school and got into an argument with one naysayer that nearly caused us to come to blows. I was beginning to see that I was the only one of my classmates to still believe in Santa. Not wanting to be anyone's fool, I again confronted my mother. In doing so I experienced one of the most traumatic events of my young life.

I approached my mother this second time with the eyes and ears of a skeptic and this time caught her trying to cover for her lies with some thin statement about the 'Spirit of Santa' being real. Although I was too young at the time to fully understand the concept of 'The Spirit' I could sense that I was asking the wrong question...I next asked her, 'Do you put the presents under the tree?' I had an epiphany. I suddenly realized that if my mother would lie to me about something so important and using the same language I had heard in reference to the 'Holy Spirit' no less, then she may have been lying about 'Him' as well. After all, I had never seen God either. I ran off into the woods and cried. I felt as though my heart had been broken. My chest burned and I felt like I had been punched in the stomach. My whole world had been shattered.

I immediately began to question everything. I went to my Sunday school teacher, my father, and my mother to try to understand how and why they were able to believe in God. After having been told more than once that it was a matter of faith, I realized that no one had actually spoken with God and that no one really had any answers. I knew that the only way to get any real answers was to die. I was so consumed with finding that truth that I would eventually place a gun to my head and consider pulling the trigger. I became very depressed and my doubts became a burden I could hardly stand to carry. I couldn't sleep at night and even began chanting nearly every waking moment to counter all the bad things my own voice was saying inside of my head. This continued for almost two years until I discovered alcohol and was finally able to enjoy a good night's sleep.

The effects of this spiritual trauma I suffered long ago reverberated through the years. In my late twenties I finally started to get a handle on the issues that arose from having lost my faith. I felt guilty because I then could see that Jesus and God had been the truth all along and that I should not have ever compared them to Santa Claus.

I have resolved to tell my children the truth about Santa the first time they ask. In doing so, I can only hope that they will never doubt what I have taught them about God. I am also careful about which churches they attend. I have no doubt that my discovering that I had been lied to about Santa was the reason that I lost my faith in God and very nearly had my life destroyed."

This was a great article written by a college aged person that points sharply to the need for parents to be honest with their children about the fantasies that have developed in our society. It is not only Santa Claus, but one has to throw in the Easter Bunny, Easter Eggs, and the "cute" little witches and warlocks that some parents think entertaining and harmless.

PUDDLE 13

MALE RETICENCE

Have you noticed that the male and female of the species appear, act, and think differently? If you haven't, you may have a serious perceptual problem. From a male perspective, the difference is all good. He is attracted to the female largely due to these differences. He is usually looking for a mate who is extremely attractive, has an impeccable personality, and who is properly submissive. Some definition may now be in order concerning these desired attributes. Attractiveness may be defined as comely in appearance and in possession of 56-26-36 dimensions. Personality attributes may include never talking to him in the same way that he talks to her, being able to negotiate with salesmen without pulling the male away from his recreational activity, and always making him feel clever, humorous, and wise. Submission means being ready to adjust her schedule on a dime to meet his impulsive whim.

Certainly God had a purpose in allowing for this differentiation between the male and the female. Likewise, the evolutionist would point to such adaptation as necessary to propagate the species. Keep in mind that we are considering human beings at this point, as a fish is a fish is a fish.

So we have the viral, sexually explosive male set up to be attracted to the submissive, passive female who is looking for a mate to protect her, provide stability in her life, and ensure family continuity. Wait just a minute! That may have been the way it used to be but we have experienced a little change over the past several years in role identification. While your mother may admit that she "chased him until he caught her," in the present day, female aggressiveness appears to have accelerated to mach levels. It is not unusual to see males cautiously peering around corridor corners in hope of avoiding the persistent young lady whose biological clock is ticking. The relatively "bad" boys are much in demand while the "nice" guys are categorized as being boring. Women are brazen in their adaptation of "explosive sexuality" and persistent in premeditated efforts to ensnare the hapless chromosomal XY. They stare shamelessly at the male's tight derriere, not considering why the muscle constriction develops as he flees desperately down the dark alleys in the vain attempt to escape the female's ferocity of chase.

Well, it is high time that a knowledgeable male "educates" women as to how most "normal" guys really are. Men are usually naturally shy. They cringe when stared at, and never go to the powder room holding hands together (unless there are other issues involved). Inside of the public restroom, they will often stand looking into the mirror on the wall for long periods of time waiting for other males to leave so that they might use the facilities in private. They never, ever, hold social conversations between toilet stalls. They are horrified, if perchance, they accidentally leave their pant's fly open and some female notices. They rarely are aware of what another fellow is wearing and certainly do not become extensively out of sorts if someone else is wearing the same pair of jeans.

Ah, you say, what about the occasional male exhibitionist? Certain aberrations do occur but even these are often over-compensators or individuals with unresolved issues. Two examples come to mind. When I was in high school, the girls and boys shared a gymnasium for physical education classes.

The girls would come from a dressing room on one side and the boys from another. One of the young men, having been involved in some horseplay prior to appearing on the floor for class, forgot his shorts, instead appearing in a fine sweatshirt and a jock strap. Unfortunately for this sensitive chap, the girls were all seated on the bleachers waiting for roll call when he came running out, bouncing a basketball. In response to the sudden verbal commotion and laugher from the grouped fairer sex, he looked down to notice his oversight. Now had this been a female, the modern young lady would have positioned the basketball strategically, hopefully would have blushed appropriately, possibly would have blown a few kisses at the boys in the stands, and would have retreated slowly to the dressing room, anticipating that a few of the young women would still be there to listen to her rendition of the exhibition. The young man, instead, was horrified. He threw the basketball down and ran as fast as he could back to the dressing room, trying manually to cover as much geography as humanly possible. He did not return to the floor and later sat in the classroom attempting to be the "invisible man."

Years later, as a freshman at Drake University, all new students had to take a perfunctory physical examination on campus. I noticed that one line awaiting entrance to the health services building was extremely long while another had only a couple of young ladies waiting. Proudly, I thought to myself, those in the long line were not paying attention, so I hurried to take my place behind the few coeds. Casually, more in an effort to meet the young ladies in line ahead of me than for information seeking, I pondered aloud, "Why is everyone staying in that long line?" The answer was soon forthcoming, "The physician screening this line is a woman and some of the fellows are too shy to be examined by her." I immediately took my position at the end of the long line. After all, we fellows have a right to our privacy.

PUDDLE 14

DOES SHE KNOW THAT IT REALLY ISN'T ME?

Every year I set up a "Birthday Breakfast Bash" for my wife and approximately thirty of her closest friends at the Edom Bakery and Grill. Annually, I struggle in an attempt to identify a little entertainment for them while they enjoy the wonderful cranberry muffins and other specialties even though I have noticed that women in a large group are usually so busy talking that they do not need clowns or acrobats.

This year was no different. I had attempted to schedule a barber shop quartet from the local community, but failed due to a scheduling conflict. Recounting this failure in my welcome address to the gathering, I then jokingly informed the ladies that I had then approached a trio of male strippers. However, I was again turned down when the lead dancer looked at the guest list and gasped, "I can't do it, my mother is going to be there and I don't want her to know what I do in my spare time!" The anticipated laughter in response to this clever comment was not forthcoming. Certainly, there were a few chuckles, but more obvious were the veiled glances around the tables. It became apparent that I had energized some suspicion that perhaps the story was not a fabrication. Perhaps one of their sons really was into the wearing of leather! I use the word "energized" since one can imagine how this revelation would have taken on a life of its own in the telling and retelling over the next few days.

Later, standing in line for the buffet behind the female assemblage, I casually, but loudly, asked the woman ahead of me, "And how is your son?" My innocent inquiry was rewarded with an equally loud and defensive response, "He is a preacher!" The retort was quickly followed by a quick confirmatory scan of others around her to make sure that they had either not heard the interchange or had cognitively grasped the response.

Next year come the dancers with a pre-arranged "Hi Mom" to some unsuspecting church lady.

PUDDLE 15

"OH, I GET IT"

The lack of awareness, more specifically "self-awareness" constitutes a large puddle all of its own. Observation of this condition brings forth a mixed reaction. Our gentle and caring nature brings forth a feeling of sympathy. If we personally have experienced the same behavior, it brings forth empathy. However, in most situations, we merely shake our collective heads and often allow ourselves a chuckle at someone else's expense.

A recent example is brought to mind. I was passed on a city street by what could only be described as a real "clunker." This car was laden with rust, a mechanical memorial to past dings from misuse and reckless positioning in parking lots. What little paint remained was faded and scratched. Its headliner dropped down, partially blocking the sight of the driver. The seat covers were ripped and stained. Do you get the picture?

Well, on the passenger side door was a large, proud, plastic advertising sign. It stated, "Need to make money? Work from Home…$500 to $5000 per week."

Incongruity!

PUDDLE 16

WHAT YOU WISHED EVERY PROFESSING CHRISTIAN WOMAN WOULD KNOW

I am always curious as to the level of self-awareness possessed by many "Christian" women in our current culture. From childhood they have been taught that lust, fornication, adultery, covetousness, and a long list of other behaviors are not only wrong, but forbidden. Their religious education would have gone further and would have indoctrinated them into the understanding that such offenses do not necessarily have to have been acted upon, but can also be comprised of a thought or fantasy. However, as soon as the transition begins to take place between latency and adolescence, many young "ladies" set themselves in seduction mode. Is this due to the exacting demands of the evolutionary process in the need to repopulate the planet? Would the reproduction of the species fail were the tenants of their religion realized? Is the teaching of young women in the churches being downplayed in the interests of current fashion trends? Is peer pressure more significant than "spiritual" guidance? Are women merely morally-flawed individuals?

Recently, I attended a meeting at which an attractive young woman got up and prayed, and prayed, and prayed. She was wearing an attractive outfit, neckline plunging to her navel, and hemline dangerously close. In answer to the anticipated but unasked question, this was noted before she started praying and as she went to take her seat. It was a little like the preacher who includes such an interesting "grab-you" story in his sermon that the teaching segment is forgotten while the anecdote is told and retold. In this case, for both male and female participants, the outfit will long be remembered, while it is only hoped that God heard her prayer.

Would the prayer have been more appropriate had she been wearing a burqa? Probably not outside of the Muslim countries, and even there it might have drawn to her the wrong type of attention if offered in mixed company.

Christian men are warned that lust of thought is as condemned as lustful action. Yet, what is a man to do, with all these seductive "ladies" running around apparently attempting to outdo each other in gaining inappropriate attention from men? Certainly, the male can look the other way, gouge out his eyeballs, flagellate himself with a baseball bat, but it just doesn't seem to be fair.

Come on "ladies," you know very well what you are doing or are attempting to do. You are trying to drive the opposite sex into sin! Well, maybe this is not a conscious motivation. Maybe you are just attempting to gain his attention so he will lust after you. Well, maybe this is too severe. Perhaps you are just warm blooded and need to have a lot of air circulation. Then again, you may be extremely uncomfortable in your exposed condition, but you are a captive of fashion.

What you need to know is that for mature men, some of the most seductive, attractive, sought after women are those who dress modestly and appropriately. They are the ones that men like to be seen with and are not the object of ridicule in conversation after each staging. Certainly men like titillation, but they also appreciate sophistication and female self-confidence. To expose all is to expose a real heavy dose of self-depreciation.

PUDDLE 17

WAYSIDE RELATIONSHIP

Being a coffee aficionado is not an easy life in the fast food world. One finally finds a place that serves respectable java, only to have it take on an entirely different quality on its next visit. It is a little like the beverage available at my present place of employment. Slowly it starts to taste like what one imagines the seepage from a cat litter box to be, after being left out in a pouring rain.

My wife and I usually stop by various restaurants for their "senior" coffee. Usually it is fairly good and, considering it is half price, a basic tolerance has to be exerted. However, sometimes it really craters. Was it that the content of the pot was old, or was it the pot itself that was old? Was the change due to water variability, the quality of the coffee by batch, or a brewing device with fungus and mold dwelling therein?

We finally found a little outlet that was consistent in its brew. In making this discovery, however, we noticed some ancillary random practices that were not evident in other outlets of the same chain. We noticed that the young lady at the counter was not only meticulously groomed and obviously enthusiastic about her job but she did a couple of other notable things including sanitizing her hands after handling money and using a lid applicator for the tops of the cups rather than just jamming them down with her hands. This was so impressive that it merited an e-mail to the company website.

Being people of routine, the little restaurant became our stop of choice on the way to work each morning. It also earned the focus of our inquiring minds. My wife is intrusive, my curiosity is scientifically based. What really was the difference? Why did this shop have better coffee than the others, even of the same chain? We then noticed the shift manager, an industrious young Hispanic man with a ready smile. Another procedural dissimilarity, twice when our arrival coincided with the content of the pot being low, he asked, "If you have just a minute, I will brew up a new pot." We did not quibble about the distinction of whether it was the pot being brewed or the contents therein; we were just impressed that he would care enough to take the trouble to create extra work for himself.

What really made the difference? It was not the water, the coffee beans, the upkeep of the brewing apparatus; it was rather the attitude, motivation, pride, self-awareness, and relationship of the staff. It just made the coffee taste better.

Both employees consistently greeted customers with authentic smiles and what followed was relaxed interpersonal involvement. They were providing not only a product, but a service. They signaled to their customers that they were proud of their work and welcomed interaction with them. They worked diligently, but with none of the fake bustle and nerve-wracking din projected by many food service staff. They related well because they were obviously comfortable with themselves and with others.

Do these characteristics always lead to well-brewed coffee? Probably not, but they do build great relationships. So some morning when your home-brewed coffee takes on the aroma and taste of a litter box, why not go out and try to find a couple of young people behind a counter who would enjoy serving you?

PUDDLE 18

RELATIONSHIPS OF ANOTHER SORT

"Living Bridges" is what I call them. What I am referring to here is the affection that we have for others of short acquaintance. The Bible clearly teaches that we should love the Lord our God and our neighbor as ourselves. Popular culture, on the other hand, seems to teach that erotic, lustful love is the standard for modern society. One popular soap opera to which I became temporarily addicted required that the viewer really concentrate on who was sleeping with whom in any particular episode. The attraction to this seedy drama was not to the animalistic behaviors of the characters in the drama, rather it was more to challenge myself to predict which sewer line the story would next flow into and how I personally would have written the script to make it even more shocking.

Regardless, I have always been fascinated with the affectionate relationships of an agape quality that my wife develops with individuals scurrying around in their attempts to remain strangers, but who fall within her scope and focus of association. They are almost immediately "captured" and charmed into becoming friends who may or may not ever cross paths with her again.

During a recent work trip to Milwaukee, Wisconsin, I maintained an informal record of the development of such episodes, some of which will be recounted here. I suspect that the power of a loving personality is at play here as I certainly do not have the ability or the desire to make similar conquests. If the fact be known, I do not particularly like people, especially those that take the form of loud invasive children. But having made this side comment, this "puddle" is not about me, but about the "living bridges" that my wife develops.

The first contact on this trip was a young man who we will call "Ken" for the purposes of anonymity. We were closing out a living estate and found his ad in the yellow pages. He described himself as a fellow who buys "stuff, the more unusual the better." Upon first contact, my wife developed a friendship with this bright young man who was warm, kind, and authentic. They were almost immediately on a first name basis, laughing and joking about life's pressures and learning about each other's foibles and personality characteristics. A couple of weeks after Ken's first buy of several insignificant items from us, my wife learned that one of our family members had wanted several of the pieces of broken merchandise. Against my advice and better judgment, my wife jumped on the telephone and asked to repurchase them. Ken not only drove the items back to the house, but refused to take payment for them. Pretty unusual in this day and age of cut throat merchandising. Recently, Ken sat in our living room visiting with my wife and her unfriendly husband. Oh yes, spiritual faith came up as a topic, but not as sandpaper, but rather as a natural mutual interest.

The second bridge was similar, but this time it was in the service industry. My wife loves her strawberry sodas. A restaurant famous for this item in the Milwaukee area was a long driving distance across the city, so we decided to seek out a shop in a different chain. Going in, the young people at the counter claimed to have no knowledge of how to concoct such a food item. They asked one of the managers, a young lady we will call "Debbie," if she knew of this drink that my wife was requesting. Debbie smiled warmly, said that she used to make such concoctions, and proceeded to whip up the best ice cream soda that my wife had experienced in years. Evening after evening, my wife sought out Debbie, who became her "go to girl" for sodas. Debbie became a personality, someone to be treasured for her warm smile, quick recognition, and friendliness. I am certain that my wife will stop by to bid her good-bye following this stint in the badger state.

Then came "Julie," a waitress at a restaurant which has the most fabulous vegetarian omelets served on a huge plate with greasy American fried potatoes and fried onions. The first evening that we stopped, Julie worked our table. In addition to having a "waitress" mentality and a typical distain for customers, she was funny. We began to gently "needle" her, laugh with her, and "get into her head." The next time we stopped in, she was not working and the meal lacked enjoyment, although the food remained excellent. The third time we pointed her out to the hostess and asked to be seated at one of her tables. She, like Debbie, became a "person" to love and to know, another treasure for my wife's informal field of honor and respect, another person at her gate who was not allowed to remain a stranger.

The list could go on to include the Fed-Ex employee who went well beyond his job description in assisting my wife with her multiple shipments; the laundry owner who agreed to take special care of some old shawls of sentimental value; the two garbage workers who received an ice cold Dr. Pepper from my wife as they were loading up more than sixty bags of heavy refuse from the wet basement.

What is the point of this narrative? It shows that people, even those hardened by our society and culture, still respond to the interest and love of someone who recognizes them as brothers and sisters in Christ or those who might be subject to future adoption. I am not referring to a phony attempt to lure someone to a particular church organization (which might actually drive those seeking God further from the truth) or even trying to convert strangers to a saving faith (God does that); but rather, meeting a human need to give love to others and to receive the satisfaction of returned affection.

These "Living Bridges" do not have to have story lines or known conclusions. While waiting in the car this morning as my wife dashed into an establishment to purchase a cup of coffee, I noted an elderly lady take a table against the window. She appeared somber, even a little depressed, as she stared blankly out into the parking lot. It was obvious that she was not looking forward to starting her day's responsibilities, whatever they might have been. Then I saw my wife walk by with a quick smile and a spoken "Good Morning." I watched the stranger's expression as her eyes followed her new acquaintance out the door. First there was surprise, even puzzlement, but then the reward; a warm smile in return.

This is what it is all about, loving our Lord and our neighbor as ourselves. I could go on and on as these special relationships develop, but I would wager that you are doing the same thing and experiencing the same joy.

PUDDLE 19

RACCOONS

Strange are some of the people that one meets standing in line at a superstore. They are so much different than this observer! I was in one of those 20 products or fewer checkout lines with a cart filled with exactly 19 items when I noticed an elderly gentleman behind me, awkwardly holding onto a large fifty pound sack of something in one hand and a small container in the other. Since he did not have a cart on which to balance the weight, I suggested that he cut in line ahead of me so that he might place his heavy sack on the counter. He smiled his appreciation, thanked me, and then placed what turned out to be a bag of cat food and an economy size bottle of pain reliever down. He turned to me with an apologetic look and seemed to feel that he needed to offer an explanation for his purchase. I had already formed my own opinion but had nowhere to turn so we developed eye contact and the explanation commenced. He had a yard full of pet raccoons which he fed. He explained that dog food was much more expensive then cat food so he used the latter, obviously in significant quantities. He then was greeted by the clerk and our friendly conversation concluded. You wonder about the big bottle of pain reliever? No, I suspect it was not for a particular raccoon with a splitting headache. Rather, it was probably for the kind animal lover who undoubtedly receives a din of condemnation from next door neighbors for enticing raccoons to his backyard. They are handsome animals.

PUDDLE 20

BICKERING AS A PASTIME

Frequently, my wife and I stage "fun" arguments in the presence of strangers, not only to pass the time but also to watch reactions. We often default to this routine when we are waiting for a clerk or other such contact to complete some transaction and the process is taking too long.

We were recently waiting in line at a medical check-in desk at a local clinic. The clerk was attempting to make some mindless conversation as she filled out duplicates of equally mindless forms. She glanced up at my wife without any apparent interest and opined that she had seen her around and ended the comment by referring to her as Mrs. Vierkant. I interjected the comment that my wife had only purchased the surname and that I was actually the one born with it. I further indicated that my wife had paid a four dollar fee for a license to acquire my name. At this point my wife corrected my statement by saying, "No, you were the one who paid the four dollars." As the fake argument progressed, the clerk stopped her paperwork, did not raise her eyes to look at us, but stared straight ahead. One could only surmise that she was thinking to herself, "You meet all types on this job."

Later the same afternoon, my wife and I closed a small savings account and walked it over to an adjacent bank in order to take advantage of a slightly higher interest premium. The

"Lobby-Clerk," yes that was the title on his identification badge, was obviously new and nervous. He completed his mound of meaningless documentation on a computer, printed it out, and then handed it over for signatures. The process had only taken about fifteen minutes, but was enough to bore the cranky old couple waiting to move on to something really exciting such as grocery shopping. I signed two places, initialed another, and handed it over to my wife. She glanced at the document and leveled a feigned angry look at the poor "would-be" bank executive. "You typed in his name in front of and on top of mine. I was the one who earned this money. Why would you do such a thing?" I immediately jumped in and retorted, "My dear, it is because traditionally, in a patriarchy, men are seen as being much more responsible and his documentation was completely correct!" We then both went silent and stared intently at the young man who was nervously rolling a pen around in his hand, anxiously searching our faces to pick up a clue as to how serious this situation had become, while he slowly rocked back and forth in his "secretarial" level chair. My wife then demanded to know, "Who owns this bank?" The young man went into a disjointed explanation of ownership, naming two males. My wife's response, "I notice that you did not mention any wife involved. Are both these men single?" The "Lobby-Clerk" then hastened to explain that he was certain that they were married, but that he did not know all the details, and that he would be happy to redo the paperwork to our satisfaction. At this point, we started laughing and the harassed young man appeared as though he was eager to get rid of us so that he could visit the male counterpart of a "powder room."

Our most recent episode took place at a local franchise-style restaurant. For some reason, when we patronize this rather low-class establishment, the inept hostess always seats us in a narrow booth adjacent to a walkway. Not to be debited to her account of functionality, but she does not seem to notice that both my wife and I could really benefit from a weight loss program. So in order to squeeze into the bench seat by the fixed top table both of us have to "suck in our guts," to express the concept in rather uncouth terms. This time, my wife would have none of it. We were both tired, having put in an honest day's work. My wife turned to "Pricilla" (probably not her name, but you get the image) and declared, "There is no way that we can comfortably squeeze in there." Seizing the opportunity, I glared at the hostess and said, "Yes, the space is much too narrow for my wife." Then the fun began as my comment led to an extensive discussion regarding who was the culprit that could not slide into the narrow space. Finally, we were taken to what appeared to be a table for full grown adults and the hostess scurried away making eye contact with neither of us and obviously feeling very awkward for contributing to a verbal altercation that she did not realize was all in fun. The high point was when we had finished dining on something that was of mysterious origin, and we were walking toward the exit, the hostess jumped up and held the door open for us. I thanked her and especially expressed appreciation that she could find a seat large enough to accommodate my wife. The little girl stared straight ahead, grasped her menus, and sighed, "Good Night!"

It does pass the time and makes this challenging or "challenged" couple memorable.

PUDDLE 21

MISCOMMUNICATION HAS CONSEQUENCES

Recently, the new administrator of the small Christian two-year college where I teach as an adjunct obviously wanted to get off to a good start by rearranging offices, installing new carpet, having walls painted, etc. Having taught courses at the school for over 20 years, such renovation was often precluded by budgetary constraints. When it was first announced during a semester break, a few of us groaned. We had become acclimated to our old offices. We had long ago forgotten how worn our little "closets of refuge" had become. We certainly dreaded packing up years of accumulated materials that we had squirreled away because we felt that "someday we might need them."

Bowing to the demands of my compulsive personality, I arrived on campus soon after the doors of the educational building were unlocked. Having no idea where I was being moved, or even whether as an adjunct I would have an office to move into, I wheeled box after box of material out to my pickup. (Yes, almost every Texan has a truck.) Having almost completed the job and feeling every muscle in my body strained to the limit, two employees from maintenance happened by and expressed their curiosity as to my efforts. I learned that I would indeed be moving to a small room in another building and the

way was "made straight for me." Opening the door, I saw a
room that was storage with a capital "S." Well, I unloaded the
"stuff" and making multiple trips, wheeled it across campus to
the new locale. I was told to place the accumulated "stuff" that
had been stored in my new "office" into the hallway while my
"stuff" took possession of the area.

However, I had to make one final walk to "my" old office,
not so much to bid it adieu, but more to see what changes were
being made as the contractors pounced on it as soon as the last
torn piece of scrap paper was removed. The old gray painted
bookcase that had lined one wall had already been ripped out.
The old rusting steel desk was lying on its side in the hallway. A
young Hispanic painter was proudly looking over the new gray
color painted on the cinder block tiles. The old green torn carpet
still proudly adhered to the floor as if to say, "Some things go
reluctantly".

I speak no Spanish and the young man spoke very little
English. I commented, "It looks good." To this rather bland
comment, the painter answered, "Yes, she wanted it porple."
Assuming that he was saying, "purple," the next occupant may
have to have a vivid imagination.

PUDDLE 22

WHO FEELS AWKWARD?

On a recent trip to Springfield, Illinois, I stopped at a Wal-Mart store to pick up a few groceries to take to the motel. It was a nice store with pleasant and helpful "associates." When I arrived at the checkout counter, a clerk about my age smiled and started scanning the purchases. I noticed that something was different, but it was not until she began packing those awkward little plastic sacks that I realized what I was observing. The lady may have been a "thalidomide baby" or had some other cause for the fact that she had only one functional arm, while the other was rudimentary. The scene became all about my feelings of discomfort. She was doing a great job. The corporation certainly was deserving in their willingness to hire an individual who had to compensate for real physical, but not emotional, restrictions. I wanted to lean forward and hold the sack open for her but this was not needed. I wanted to compliment her ability to maneuver a process which is difficult enough for individuals with two workable hands, but that would be suggesting something that she no longer saw as a problem. I wanted to stare in order to determine how she possibly could handle the check-out process so rapidly. Instead, I pretended not to notice and she continued on to the customer behind me.

Isn't it peculiar how we feel sympathy, or better, empathy for those who have overcome handicaps in life and do not really always know how to react to our own feelings? In such a case, business as usual is probably the best approach. I wonder what her response would have been had I leaned forward and said, "Let me help you with that." I am glad that I did not.

PUDDLE 23

CAPTIVE IN A PUBLIC RESTROOM

My wife and I have a real public restroom "thing." If I can avoid using such a facility, I most certainly will do so. We have experienced some pretty terrible locations, such as one state supervised "rest stop" that caused my spouse to return to the car after merely peering in the doorway. She informed me that the floor was so filthy that anyone walking in would probably have their shoes stick to the cement. As she was informing me of this condition, I heard her exclaim, "Oh No!" Three young teenage girls were walking toward the building barefooted. Hardly the non-interventionist, my better-half jumped from her seat and stopped the young ladies just as they were about to enter. They looked at her strangely, as if to say, "What business is this of yours?" They then entered the facility without an apparent concern in the world.

When our children were small, my wife would approach such facilities well-armed with a large can of disinfectant and stern warnings on restroom survival. Do you ever wonder why public restrooms are often out of tissue paper? Well, the truth is that my wife and our six kids were just there and each seat had been carefully covered with layers of tissue.

Anyway, there are times when such necessary visits are both awkward and humorous. Several years ago, I entered a restaurant restroom only to notice that the facility did not have the usual male-oriented fixtures. Just then I heard female voices approaching, so I ducked into a stall and was terrorized while two women stood within a couple of feet of me talking at length about another woman who apparently was the butt of their ridicule (no pun intended). Finally, they entered two adjoining stalls and I dashed for the door. Thank goodness that there were four stalls. I exited the restaurant, got in the car, and said to my wife, "Let's get out of here." Was there a sign on the door? Probably, but perhaps I was preoccupied with other thoughts.

Then, the situation struck again, only this time for my wife. We were driving into Arkansas from the North on highway 67 and spotted a state rest stop. I must admit, this facility was a wonderful exception to the rule. It was a newer building, stocked with shelves of free brochures, and supervised by two ladies who were obviously proud of their location and its condition. We were directed to the restrooms and then invited to have a complimentary cup of coffee on our way out. Then the confusion began. The cleaning process was to lock two restrooms for cleaning while two others were made available. My wife entered the first facility which was obviously marked "Men." Her later excuse was that she was in conversation with the ladies and had not read the sign. I hollered at her to come back out, much to the amusement of the bystanders, and then went in myself. Almost immediately, a large van with several males arrived and crowded into the men's room. While sipping my coffee and awaiting the return of my wife from the "powder room," the arrival of men did not stop. Considering most male facilities have only one stall, my wife could have been very annoying to the line of men who might have been waiting.

The lesson from this puddle: read signs on public restroom doors.

PUDDLE 24

SHEEP

I have nothing against sheep as critters. In fact, as a young man, I had a small flock of Suffolks which impressed me much more favorably than the one goat that roamed with them. On the other hand, I am much more critical of sheep of the human variety and find the few human "goats" that I run into like a breath of fresh air.

It is one thing to be classified as a "sheep" because one lacks courage or does not want to "kick against the pricks." It is another thing to be merely apathetic. Have you noticed that there seem to be many more male sheep of a human variety than female? One of the complaints that I hear so frequently among young, unmarried, female, college students is that men of courage, reliability, and substance are difficult to find. Could it be that our "shack up rate" has grown so rapidly just for this reason? Young ladies do not want to cast their temporal life lot with a "loser." If they could be sure that the male would be there for them through thick and thin, perhaps they would be more demanding of a ring on the left paw before becoming "involved." Of course cynics might say that some women are so desperate to have a man that they will go to any lengths to be with one.

It is entirely another thing to just be a mindless follower of the latest fad. Such a person is not even a functional critter, rather he or she is definitely a dumb animal. One of the indicators of being a low functioning sheep is the fad of pot-bellied, middle-aged men strutting around with their caps on backwards. As they slap each other on the derrière and grunt, "Hey Man," they look ridiculous and degrade themselves. As in many developing fads, there seems to be an evolution or perhaps better phrased a "devolution" in etiquette. Recall the gentleman of the 20s doffing his hat in the presence of a lady? Then, in the 30s and 40s, the man of breeding touched his headgear and slightly bowed to the representative of the fairer sex. Now, the personified sheep do not even remove their "give-me" caps in restaurants and it might be speculated that such keep their cranial areas warm at night on the pillow. Well, perhaps such a "man" is just a clod rather than a sheep. The wooly animal comes on the scene after observing a smirking professional athlete walk around with his cap reversed. Thereafter, and following several trips to the mirror, the sheep has his "style."

I was driving down an urban street the other day to see one of these sheep driving a fine convertible automobile with the top down. He was turning onto the thoroughfare from a side street, facing the glare of a setting sun. His face was puckered, his left hand was in a shading position, he obviously was valiantly trying to see where he was going, while his cap with a long, functional bill was turned straight back. What can one say but, "Baa, Baa, Baa"?

PUDDLE 25

ANGEL WINGS

Every once in a while you hear a comment made that is a real "head scratcher." Was the person making the statement as a joke or was his understanding of reality way out in space somewhere? I heard two "over the hill" athletes pontificating on a little known radio sports program one night and somehow they floundered their way into the arena of "mortality." One commented, "Well, we never know when God will need another angel." Loosely analyzed, his comment had something to do with not knowing how long someone would live, couched in a fatalistic viewpoint on life. Certainly, I thought, he really is not suggesting that he believed that upon death, we become angels! Now, there was no theological consideration of whether we become good or bad angels or any discussion of redemption, pathways, or other scriptural hurdles. In making reference to this rather strange comment to my wife that evening, I opened myself up for a lecture on how many children are entertained with fanciful concepts and that it is the responsibility of adults to correct such misconceptions when discovered. Apparently she had been taught by her grandmother that shoulder blades were the foundational infrastructure for the anticipated attachment of wings following our earthly transition. My response, "Certainly she was jesting!"

But then I began to think of the other unsubstantiated and confusing concepts that parents, both believing and unbelieving, pass on to their children. Santa Claus, the Easter Rabbit, cupcakes with imagined depictions of Christ's face, and who knows what other fantasies are set forth without thoughtful consideration.

But it is a small step from confused, yet entertaining concepts, to our own hang-ups about those things spiritual. For example, I have several old, worn-out Bibles taking up storage space as I cannot bring myself to dispose of because they are "Holy Scripture." Haven't any of you received a depiction of Christ through some advertising gimmick and could not just toss it in the wastebasket? In fact, I will go out of my way to remove something that has been placed inadvertently on a Bible. Where did this need arise? Who was my teacher? But no, shoulder blades are not the connection points for angel wings and, no, we do not become angels following our departure from this life and yes, I don't think the comment was a critical issue on the success or lack thereof of this particular sports show.

PUDDLE 26

THE PIG WHO EXPIRED

Several years ago I had an old car that had literally "bitten the dust." Trying to figure out the best way to dispose of it, as its trade-in value was negligible, I happened across an advertisement by a charitable organization that offered to take donations of old vehicles, running or not. I also recognized that this particular organization was the same one that had recruited one of my best staff away a few years prior. However, not being one to hold a grudge and just wanting to get rid of the car that had not been good even in its "day," I called the number in the advertisement. Fate had it that the voice that answered was the familiar one of the young lady who had formerly worked under my supervision. Obviously, she did not have caller identification and there was no doubt that she did not recognize my voice. The conversation commenced, "I read an ad in the paper that your organization will accept old vehicles and give a receipt for a donation." The response was, "Certainly, we have a contract with a local towing company that will pick it up at your home and we will authorize a receipt." My comment, "Well, this is a pretty special vehicle; it may be difficult to tow." Her response, "I am sure we can handle it. What kind of vehicle is it?" Bending the truth a bit, I said, "Well, it is a truck." Without missing a beat, the agency representative allowed that it could be handled. I then hesitated and said, "Well, there is one additional consideration." Patiently, but with a little caution in her voice, she said, "What is that?" I responded, "The pig." Her response, "Pig?" I said, "Yeah, but it isn't going to be too much trouble as it is dead; in fact, it has been that way for several months. I just didn't have anywhere to unload it." The communication gapped for a few minutes and the wary lady asked, "Who did you say that you were?" Upon identification, we had a good laugh, at her expense. But oh, how I wish that I really had an old unserviceable truck with a pig on it, just to see how the scenario would have played out.

PUDDLE 27

THE HOTEL

In previous books, I have expounded, to the reader's painful experience, some of the rich stories that originate in motels and hotels. It seems that the "cheaper" the establishment, the richer the story minefield becomes. Probably the best place for the observer of the ridiculous is to sit in the "free" breakfast rooms of such establishments.

However, in this puddle, I will be following a more serious observational line. It was an "educational moment" for me and hopefully, it will be of spiritual growth food for you also.

My wife was attending a professional conference in Austin, Texas, at an up-scale hotel, unlike something that we would stay at using our own dime. I had prepared for a boring time in the room by taking along reading material, my ever-present laptop, and anticipating watching some of the television news programs. Unfortunately, but very predictably, my wife had some "assignments" for me to complete while she completed her assigned task. "Will you preview the MacArthur book, *Standing Strong*, and decide whether it is one that we would like to read together in our morning devotionals?" My response was curt and took the form of a snarl. "I have a lot a stuff that I want to read today, I just want to kick back, get out of the box for a while, and even possibly watch some mindless television. I will do it later." As soon as she left the room, I wimped out, carefully rationalizing that I really wanted to go down to get a free cup of coffee anyway and that I could just as well take the book along to take a look at it. As is the case in many of the MacArthur books, the hook was set as soon as I started reading and the coffee was flowing freely. Finally, I tucked it under my arm and headed to the fancy glassed-in elevator to return to our second floor digs. Just as the door was closing, a well-dressed individual squeezed through the door and punched the top floor button which would set the elevator to take him to the executive suites. I was of little interest to him as an individual, but his eyes focused on the book under my arm. "What are you reading, he inquired?" I responded, "*Standing Strong* by John MacArthur." He seemed suddenly genuinely interested and said, "I know that name from somewhere." I quickly filled him in as to where on the internet he could find the website to obtain books and materials from the *Grace to You* program. Almost immediately, the elevator door opened, and I took my departure.

"So what," you may be thinking? Thousands of people probably experience casual conversations in a hotel elevator each day if they are not busily ignoring each other.

But let's put some of the circumstances together or as one might say, "Let's background this a little." I have found it very awkward, unnatural, and challenging to talk to anyone about the Lordship of Christ. I am really turned off by people who get in my face and either want to give me a tract or want to inquire whether I am "saved." The witnessing varieties of motto sweatshirts do nothing for me other than to make me suspicious of motivations. It is this mind-set that causes me to be very clumsy talking to others about the Faith to which I ascribe. I am also under the impression that in a "witnessing" interaction, a transaction must be completed rather than entering and leaving an incomplete loop. I also, by nature, like to avoid situations in which I might cause someone to question his/her own

"Christian" belief paradigm, if my interpretation of scripture differs slightly from their own. Let a Lutheran be a Lutheran and a Dutch Reformed be a Dutch Reformed as long as they are obedient to the Lordship of Christ and do not place cultural values above scriptural teaching.

But the elevator incident provided me with a new insight. Was it coincidence that my wife pushed me into reviewing a book when I wanted to do something else? Was it just coincidental that the hotel had some excellent coffee in a location that would be convenient to sit close to the pot and read a book? Was it just a fluke that this affluent appearing gentleman must have seen me reading the book in the lounge and just happened to join me in the elevator going up to our respective rooms? The book, by the way, was partially concealed under my arm. Was it just that he was a gregarious individual who liked to start conversations on elevators with strangers? Was he searching for a contact with a believer? Was he just seeking something of interest to answer some of his questions? Certainly there was a 99% chance that he forgot our interchange as soon as he reached his floor. But what if he didn't? He could be entering into years of rich spiritual experience.

I have discovered during the past few years that there are many individuals who are seeking contact with servants under the Lordship of Christ. However, they want contacts that are respectful, non-threatening, and non-proselyzing. They have become burned out with the blare and manipulation of the "church builders" and just want to quietly and figuratively be touched by another believer. So, instead of forcing issues, trying to psychologically manipulate and quantatively recruit, you might just throw a seed up into the air and allow the Holy Spirit to plant it in the fertile soil of belief. There is plenty of space left in that garden.

PUDDLE 28

HELLO STRANGER

Walking into the local post office recently, I was hailed by the driver of a parked truck with a hearty and friendly "Hi there!" A rather personal flow of comments started and all at once stopped with an awkward and painful silence. It was obvious that the speaker had suddenly realized that I was someone other than who he initially thought I was. Trying to allay his embarrassment, I continued the conversation by commenting on the smooth sound of his diesel engine and telling him that it was good to see him again. Watching out of the corner of my eye, I saw him rapidly driving away, slapping his head with his hand. He didn't even check his postal box.

This situation probably has happened to you. Someone walks up to start a conversation and you are desperately looking for clues as to who they are and how to carry on a friendly conversation. Sometimes, when they recognize your discomfort, the situation will be intensified by the comment, "You don't remember me, do you?" The natural prevaricated response, "Oh sure I do, it is just that I have aged and you have remained so young!"

I was in a grocery store several years ago when an attractive checker smiled and said, "Do you remember me?" This time I was more honest and admitted that I remembered her, but could not recall her name. She stated that she had been a student in one of my classes several years prior, but then gave me a generous out. "Well, you probably would not remember me since I have changed my hairstyle." I grabbed on to this and made my less than gracious exit.

Sitting in a medical clinic waiting room the other day, it happened again. I recognized a woman from a past employment, but could not remember her name. I deliberately did not make eye contact with her and hoped that she would not see me sitting there. She walked by a couple of times without apparently noticing me but, upon leaving from her appointment, she stared right at me, walked over and said, "Hello, I did not see you over here." We shook hands and she walked off. I was thinking, "Well, that went ok, I was not placed in a situation where I would have to struggle with introducing her to someone." Suddenly, she came walking back to where I was sitting. She apologized and said, "You know, I remember you, but I cannot remember your name." I gave her this piece of information; she smiled, and walked off. Now there was a lady comfortable with herself and in many ways much more honest than I was in the situation.

Here are some interesting comments that could be made to defuse some situations:

1. "Who are you? I don't think I know you!" (This might be a little on the harsh side.)
2. "Certainly good to see you again, it has been a long time, I would stay and visit a little but my wife has her hand stuck in my car door and I have to unlock it for her." (This comment may be a little over the top.)
3. "Hey, are you coming on to me?" (This might give the wrong impression.)
4. "Move on you pervert!" (This comment would not be very friendly.)
5. "Nice to meet you little girl, are you here alone?" (This comment might get the stranger arrested on the spot.)

The point is, try to have some empathy for the friendly soul making the error. We have all had those times at various places. Sometimes playing it out to avoid embarrassment is the best approach. Other times, I like the honesty of the woman in the medical clinic; just admit that you cannot remember a name or made a mistake in the initial identification and then get a good laugh together at the awkwardness of the situation.

PUDDLE 29

CASEROLES THAT FREEZE WELL

Let me assure you that I have nothing against the lowly casserole. Being a vegetarian, the combination concoctions are one of the staples of life and my wife is an artist in their preparation. However, I have also noticed that the casserole can take on stealth characteristics when in the hands of a prowling widow or divorcee.

What usually happens almost immediately after the grieving male returns to his empty home after losing the love of his life to the Holy Transition? The casserole appears. Sometimes the arrival is above reproach. Perhaps a church group wants to provide support during the time of sorrow. Sometimes there is not a calculated hook buried deep under the mushrooms. Sometimes the hook has a well anchored-line still attached. I speak not as an individual without empathy, but as a scientist and an observer of female behavior.

There are variations in the motivation behind the process. Sometimes widows are just plain lonely and are looking for someone to live with for the rest of their lives. Even in this case, the assumed target must calculate how many times the fisherwoman has been widowed when reaching out to receive the still warm bowl. Once or twice might be ok, but if it is more, he must be certain to check the seasoning. With divorcees though, remember they have learned the ropes of disposable products which don't necessarily have to be made in China.

So there comes the anticipated knock at the door. The widower attempts to develop an optimistic expression, opens the door, and sees the steaming casserole held by a kindly appearing older woman with dyed red hair, toreador pants, and a tight-fitting high school cheerleader's sweatshirt. His eyes shift to the steam, is it really emanating from the proffered food? Expertly, the visitor offers condolences and then looks over the recipient's shoulder to evaluate the condition of the window dressings and to make an initial assessment of redecorating needs. She thinks to herself, "What is it with the ballerina pictures? My first project would be to change them out with photos of my cats."

The widower is informed that she will be back again in a few days with a little more food and at that time she will have time to stay for a visit. The widower retreats into his home, pulls the shades closed, and locks the windows. In the evenings he sits with all the house lights off and does not answer the telephone or the frequent knocking on the door. Alas, the casserole is finished, the groceries are depleted, and he cautiously walks to his car. Upon arrival at the grocery store, he senses that his grocery cart is moving without any effort on his part. Startled, he glances sidewise to realize that the predator has grasped part of the cart handle. She says, "Imagine running into you here, let me help you in making your grocery selections; products can be very confusing." You know the rest of the story, she begins to make evening meals, attends church with him, and they are labeled a "couple."

It is interesting to join in the gamesmanship of the woman on a search and capture mission. First, the male must be aware that there are no rules or parameters in this exercise. Even though the male may be vulnerable and the woman either desperate or manipulative, it does not follow that the woman lacks a robust self-concept. Remember, how we see ourselves is largely determined by how we imagine others perceive us. "Certainly," she thinks, "Did you notice how he looked at me? These toreador pants are really catching his attention!" Women are much more into themselves than men. You can check this out by watching women as they parade through the public square. Notice the slight, frozen smile that rarely leaves their faces? Men are more honest. Sometimes they wear a frown when they go about their work. Sometimes they have little facial affect. But women always have that little bird-eating smile. Men dress for comfort, work requirement, or legal obedience. Women dress to be noticed and then appear embarrassed when they receive the desired gaze.

I have tested these observations occasionally, looking for exceptions to behavior. Sometimes the confirmation comes when one is not set up for observation. I was in a grocery store recently looking at the insanely expensive dairy creamer in the fancy bottles that my wife uses when she takes coffee breaks at her employment. Male readers know the drill, "It is in a fancy bottle with a cute little pink cap and it must state 'fat free' and must not have its inner seal missing." This was all fine and good until I learned that there are about 35 such products with "cute little pink caps" on them. So the picture: older gentleman, staring through cooler doors, looking befuddled; dressed rather sloppily, but wearing socks and not scratching any part of his anatomy; no wedding band, seems to have his own teeth, could be shaped up if he had the right woman, and must have had some sort of income or else he would not be searching through the expensive section of the dairy case. Suddenly, elbowing her way past other shoppers, this woman appears, apparently on a mission, and it isn't of self-destruction. Yes, the frozen smile, had all her teeth, attractive, too young to be a widow, no wedding band (just some calloused knuckles), no rug-rats hanging on her cart, fingernails professionally done, no gaudy rings, and nice perfume. The frozen smile changed to seduction. "I noticed that you are having difficulty finding something. I don't work here, but I realize how difficult it is to locate some items." The game was on. I smiled back at her and allowed that sometimes it takes a little adjustment when a man has to shop by himself. I avoided describing the product as having a "cute little cap," rather referring to it by brand name and content. She located the product, handed it to me, made eye contact, smiled coyly and said, "See you around." Since that time, my wife locates the "insanely expensive creamer" while I avoid dark corners among the green beans.

Probably an even more flagrant "Fisherwoman" contact took place while I was sitting innocently in my car after having walked through an open house sponsored by a realty firm. Two elderly women exited. They spotted this old guy sitting in his car, seemingly having no place to go and no hurry to do so. One peeled off, walked directly up to my car and tapped on the driver's side window. I rolled it down cautiously, thinking that perhaps I was blocking someone's driveway. She smiled and said, "Saw you sitting here all by yourself and just wanted to tell you that I really like your car." I returned her smile and responded intelligently, "I do too, that is why I bought it." She looked a little taken aback, seemed to lose her nerve, and walked quickly away." It was obvious that she did not want to waste a casserole on me.

So, fellows, be always on your guard. They are out there; they prowl day and night, looking for the hungry, the defenseless, the unattached male.

PUDDLE 30

TABASCO SAUCE

Having been raised by a "Lord's Day" father, I still feel very uncomfortable with Sunday shopping. Oh yes, there are contradictions in that I will patronize a restaurant on the first day of the week and in cases of absolute necessity, my wife will pick up a few items from the drug or grocery store. This was one of those days. My mother-in-law was desperate to replace a broken alarm clock, so my wife decided that such a purchase was justified on "humanitarian grounds." And since she was going anyway, would it be ok to pick up some fresh broccoli and black beans for supper? It is amazing how when you are going to violate your conscience anyway, there are always little tasks that can be added. I was unhappy, but since I had to purchase gasoline anyway, we could just as well do it all at once. I dropped her off at the grocery section while I drove across the parking lot to fill up my gas tank. When I walked in, I noticed that she was still at customer service, which was yet another little task added to the "Great Violation." I finally got her past the broccoli and the black beans were safely in the cart, but not until a long discussion had taken place as to whether the purchase should be made of beans in oil, or beans in water. The decision was made to take one of each.

At this time, I noticed a woman in distress. Rather, she noticed me and asked that I reach a bottle of Tabasco sauce that happened to be beyond her reach on a top shelf. This annoyed me further, not only because I was now conducting more labor on the "Lord's Day," but also because the little lady was busy talking on her cell phone. How rude can people be? Put the blasted telephone away and do your shopping. Have you ever noticed that some walk into shops talking on the devices and do not even pause in their conversations at check-out? Rather, they do the shoulder hug thing, trying to sign for their credit card while holding their purses. Anyway, I graciously walked over and reached a bottle of the product for her. She interrupted her conversation long enough to ask that I take down a second bottle also. So here I stand in a crowded aisle of people who should not be shopping on Sunday anyway, in front of a lady who will not stop talking on her cell phone, and who did not have a shopping cart with her. I handed her one bottle and she recognized her dilemma. She tried to place one bottle in her jacket pocket, but it was too small. She looked pleadingly at me while I shot a glance over toward my wife who mouthed, "You shouldn't be shopping on Sunday anyway." Immediately, I had to resist two impulses. The first was to hurl a bottle of the sauce at my smirking wife. That was easy to handle as I would not want to have to pay for a broken bottle. The second impulse was more difficult to fend off. As an astute observer of female attire, I recognized that since the woman was not going to put her phone down and since her pockets would not accommodate the product and since she obviously was not going to give up on two bottles when her only free hand could grasp one, there was only one possibility left. The woman was obviously proud of her ample cleavage. The bottle could be secured there before she could even press her redial button. I hesitated, glanced at my wife, did some rapid consideration, and placed both bottles back on the shelf at a height that was convenient to the lady. I then turned and walked away, while the woman chatted on, never considering the meandering thoughts of a grumpy old man.

PUDDLE 31

POSSESSION IS NINE POINTS OF THE LAW

It is a little amazing how possessive we can become of inconsequential objects, places, or relationships in our lives. At this writing, I am sitting in a "cubical" in a public library experiencing angst at a lady who is sitting approximately two hundred feet away in my favorite spot. Certainly, it is a public location and I have no particular control over it, but that spot is just comfortable. From its location I can watch patrons arriving through the front door and observe needful ladies pouring over the pulp romantic books on a stand nearby...you know the kind that all seem to have a bare-chested man and a horse on the cover. I wish that my publisher would place such a cover on one of my efforts. It might sell better! This morning I had possession of the sought after spot and watched with unmitigated satisfaction as the lady in question glared at me and sat down at an "inferior" location. However, I made the mistake of leaving for a brief period and upon my return she had regained territorial rights. She even had her back to the bare-chested men, so that is not her hang-up.

Then we come to parking places. Have you ever noticed that we all have our favorites? My father would leave for church almost a half hour early so that he could back his car in a slot across from the front door but, more importantly, locate under a wonderful shading oak. It can totally spoil your whole evening if you return home and find someone parked in "your" space. You have a tendency to want to park behind the offender, wait for them to return to their car, and then demonstrate your dominance as you squeeze in even before they have totally vacated the spot.

I have never desired a particular place to sit in a church. All that is important to me is that I sit on the end of a pew so if the preacher becomes too caught up with himself, I can head out the back door. However, I have experienced the fierce possessiveness of location in visiting some churches, even to having a person of Christian grace stand in the aisle and glare until I moved over. Granted, there are some downers in sitting on the aisle of a pew in that church women squeezing past you to sit in the middle of a pew are too often well nourished and there becomes a knee placement problem.

In restaurants, I am fairly flexible. I prefer not to sit near nerve wracking children, groups of verbally competitive young women, or at a table near an unventilated public restroom. There is something about the hostess placement choices in some establishments that calls for further research. What is their reasoning for placing you at a particular table? Do they judge you by socioeconomic class, anticipated manners, potential tips for a favorite employee, age, weight, eye color (might be impacted you know...Puddle #5)?

As an adjunct instructor, you are pretty much near the bottom of the pecking order in the college hierarchy. This results in being moved into unfavorable office locations, if you have such a benefit at all. Currently I am located in what appeared to have been a junk-room outside of a "real" office. However, the occupant of the "real" office has to walk through my territory, in order to get into his digs. This makes neither of us happy. I occasionally walk back over to my "old" office and just stand in the hallway and look sadly at what has been removed from me. No, I was not possessive, but I want the present occupant to know that I still lurk for the next "rearrangement."

You know, while I may be a little on the possessive side, I am really happy that there is someone much more possessive than I can ever be. God, in selecting me to be one of His, gave me as a gift to His Son, our Lord, to be placed in His sheepfold, and I will continue to be with Him forever. Isn't it wonderful that the Trinity is the utmost in possessiveness of those in their keeping?

PUDDLE 32

HIS GLORY

It was a wet, cold, gloomy morning, still before sunrise and we were just arriving at my wife's school, when I turned to her and expressed a thought that had been on my mind. "Sue, I have been thinking of the grandeur and immense power of God. How does one get this idea across to others? How can one communicate this reality in such a way that they understand and believe it?" Quite unfairly, I became intensely frustrated at what I thought to be her casual "throw away" response. "It is unbelievable," she answered. She then realized that I was being deadly serious and backed her comment down by adding, "I know, it is very difficult not only to put the concept into words, but also to communicate it in a manner that will be thought through by the listener."

What I had been thinking about was the reality that God, a Power beyond our human understanding, could "speak" all creation into existence. Just to understand not only our physical surrounding, but also our individual abilities to think, communicate, understand, and remember is way beyond our comprehension. From the smallest nerve endings to the immense mountains and oceans, God made them all through merely commanding them to appear.

I thought about the young students who are so important to me as a college instructor. How many of them really have any concept of the power and majesty of God? At this point in their youthful years, they are impressed by powerful governmental figures and the social and economic powers that govern their lives. How does one get them to look past the foreground figures and look to the Power that Satan has blinded them to? How can we help them to gaze in wonderment and awe at their Creator? How can we guide them into an understanding of the only God who was, is, and shall be forever? How can we readjust our spiritual focus so that we are always aware of His Presence and unchangeable plan for us?

Whenever I spin off into such thoughts, I attempt to analyze what the stimulus for my thoughts might have been. In this case, we had heard two really meaningful messages from two different media pastors over the previous weekend and had discussed our observation that God's message has been so absent from the pulpits of churches today and the immense responsibility that "called" pastors bear for the use of their "loaned talents." Too many are burying them in the ground while forgetting that the "Lord" is coming back for an accounting. Music and performances which He would not recognize as coming from anything other than the profane and secular culture are taking place in structures theoretically dedicated to the Lord. Car washes and social gospel replace the sacred law that remains in place, even under this age of Grace. God is not only a part of the picture, He is the only portrait.

Might I suggest that every one of us start each day with a graphic pause in our cognitive process during which we visualize God's presence, power, and justice, not only in our personal lives, but totally in the Sacred Universe. At that time, let us experience the awe and even fear that the redeemed believer should feel and then let us vow to hand this mental picture out to others. Yes, this is a process devised by a mere mortal; but it is possible to carry out through God's Grace, through prayerful communication with our Lord, and through persistence in our attempts to be guided by the Holy Spirit in our study of scripture. Will we do it every morning? Probably not, but we should. In fact, if you sign on for this project, in your frail humanity, you will probably forget it by tomorrow morning, or the next one thereafter. It is not all about who we are. Shouldn't it be just about who He is?

PUDDLE 33

THOSE CHURCH SIGNS AGAIN

I try not to get all hung up on those rather silly church signs that cheapen and distort the purpose of God's sanctuaries here on earth. The signs, like my use of the word "sanctuary," should be used more judiciously. Taking the latter first, a sanctuary is for believers to enter seeking refuge and communion with God. He, in turn, certainly does not need a sanctuary for Himself. Just as a little clarification, I feel very strongly that few sanctuaries continue to exist which provide the awe, respect, and communion that the believer seeks. Even in the old days, growing up in a teaching church which did not emphasize the sanctuary concept, worshipers entered to pray and commune. Nowadays, in the modern church movement, one is more likely to meet a rock band, people loudly visiting about their secular exploits, or preachers bellowing "Good Morning" at the start of a watered down performance. Of course, one must not forget the "movie screens" with some kid shown wrinkling his nose or posturing his derriere at the camera because the parents think it is cute.

Anyway, back to church signs, I have seen the silly, the ignorant, the confused, and the misleading. I wonder what they are supposed to accomplish? Are they "loss leaders" written by "lost leaders" which are aimed at attracting the undecided customer into their services? Are they merely a joke by some elderly donor who wants to be remembered by his sense of humor? Are they established to assure the seeker that not too much intellectually will be expected from the visitor?

I ran across another one yesterday. I try not to read them as I am basically an even-tempered individual; someone who does not want to be annoyed about the little things of life. But here it was, sticking out like a sore thumb in magnificent capital letters, with the words even spelled correctly for a change. There was not an adverb defensively modifying the verb and the grammar was straight-forward. "Merely sampling the scripture will not allow for its assimilation." My mind quaked cognitively. I didn't want to criticize the message as it was not really all that offensive, but what in the world was it saying? I guess it meant that people should not sample the Bible, but rather get right into it and read straight through Leviticus without stopping and then lean back and absorb. It certainly did not mean that the seeker should avoid skimming through scripture to find truths and directions which applied to him. Perhaps what was being said is that we, as believers, are to be persistent in our scriptural study. This could have been expressed more understandably. It could be that there were not sufficient letters in the set-up box to express the statement in this manner.

Certainly the reader can add many more obnoxious signs, such as "Soar to the heavens at morning service," or "Have you been nailed yet? Christ was for you." The last one probably was a spin-off of the question as to whether the reader had taken up "his" cross and followed "Him." However, there is something about it that makes one hope that no part of the Holy Trinity is in a reading mood when traveling by this "cute" message.

The bottom line, if you are not a believer, such a sign will have little impact on you. If you are a believer, you will want to enhance your relationship with the Lord through spiritual communication and study anyway. Ok, words have meanings. Recently, in an effort to stir up more interest by students in current news events, I asked for written answers to a few questions that I worded a little differently. One of the questions asked was who is the CEO of the Executive Branch of the Federal Government in the United States? Only a couple of students came up with the correct answer and the others were quite accusatory about the question methodology. Therefore, when I refer to "spiritual communication," I am referring to prayer of a special sort. Prayer in which the believer actually trusts that someone is listening who cares and who is not only in a relationship with us, but is fully capable of responding to our petitions and praise of Him.

PUDDLE 34

WHO YOU?

Have you ever sat in a public library or outside of a shopping mall and just watched people walk by? There are all sorts of games that might be played as we watch the stream of humanity pass. We may rate them by appearance or threat to public safety. We may use a sociological approach and try to place ourselves inside of their psyche, attempting to understand how they feel, what they think. But do you realize that there is one consideration that rarely crosses our intrusive minds, namely that if they are believers, they are our brothers and sisters in Christ, regardless of external appearances or circumstance? If they are not believers, they are the walking lost, who also just happen to be our relatives. If you believe in a literal Adam and Eve, which I do; or even if you accept the scientific theory that all humans, as we know them, originated from a small group of people in some remote part of Africa (such as the proponents of the "Out of Africa" concept) we are on the same page. In fact, some now admit that we all probably came from an original mother. I wonder whether this could have been Eve?

Regardless, it is strange how detached we are from these, our distant family members, as we watch them walk by. Our Lord wept over the plight of the multitudes, even though He had the "Big Picture." We, in turn, feel strangely disassociated from them. In fact, we strongly discourage our youngsters from becoming associated with strangers, to watch with whom they socialize in their own peer groups, and to stay away from our difficult relatives.

I am not a bleeding heart. I am not into being a sister to every Girl Scout, to use a favorite phrase of my wife's. In fact, I very much treasure being alone with my thoughts in an environment of peace and quiet. However, it is still troubling how we have forgotten that these others are related to us genetically and as a life form.

But let's take this a step further. Isn't it interesting how detached we are from each other as believers in the one true God? I really think that there are some "chosen of God" in most, if not all, Christian church denominations. However, do we really salute them when we meet them out on the street as brothers and sisters in Christ? No, even those numbers are too ungainly for us. They may be of our blood lines, they may be chosen to be with us worshiping God in paradise sometime in the future, but they still are strangers. We hear of "Christians" being slaughtered in foreign countries, but does it seem real to us? Probably enough for us to shake our heads and wonder why someone doesn't do something about it, but it is hardly family.

So we break it down to the more specific doctrines of our church denominations, sometimes following man-made rules, the origin about which we usually have very little clarity. Still no big whoopee in regard to recognition of such folks as our brothers and sisters. In fact sometimes getting to know people too well within your own church can be discouraging in itself. I am not certain that there is an institutional organization which has more political problems per member than the church, and more people attempting to slice and dice each other. Of course, most church members are closer to being sheep in the agrarian sense than being action figures.

Perhaps we should just realistically focus on the family. We certainly know the people included in this construct. No, they are not all of the same blood lines, when you consider the extended family or in-laws. No, they are not all believers, a painful reality that causes untold anguish to the redeemed. In fact, sometimes an analysis of the typical family interrelationship makes the kinship with the stranger in the public library more personal and meaningful. Other than with the conjugal pair, is there any relationship that remains meaningful? Fortunately there is; that being the relationship of the believer with his Lord and God, that will always be personal, intimate, and, by definition, everlasting.

PUDDLE 35

VANITY

Isn't it strange that we all have such a strong need for recognition and praise? Why are we so insecure that we are devastated when we are ignored or gain the sense that we are invisible in the sight of others? In sociological terms, we often suggest that our self-perception is developed by how we imagine others see us. In other words, if we are smiled at on a regular basis, we feel better about ourselves. If others avert their eyes when coming into contact with us or, even worse, grimace, we lose self confidence and take a ding to our little egos.

In the town of our present residence, there are two vanity magazines published for free distribution at local stores. They are flashy, glossy, and impressive in their volume and content. Advertisers obviously flock to have their advertisements included and often to have a little notice given to them in the general content. If you attend a high dollar charity event or are involved in some other community get together for which you dress elegantly, there is a good possibility that your picture will be included in the magazine.

Why the strong need to have one's picture displayed in a magazine that often ends up on a bathroom stand? Well, we want to be important, don't we? We want to feel good about ourselves and, in order to obtain this sensation, we must be recognized by others. Left to themselves, many must feel pretty inadequate and powerless.

It is not only the printed material but we are now dealing with the electronic social media. We put someone's name in a search engine and we soon know more about them than we ever wanted or needed to know. In fact it usually includes all sorts of personal information about them such as their ugly dog, their scrawny cat, and too often their repulsive naked body. So we add the adjective "insensitive" to "inadequate" and end up with "unremarkable."

Certainly, it is nice to walk into a restaurant and have the waitress greet you with a smile and automatically draw a cup of extra strong coffee for you without having to be asked. It is wonderful to walk into a store and have someone come over and render a warm greeting. This is just a sense of relationship however. It is not all about us and our need for recognition. Could it be that perhaps we should just squat down on our hunches by the fire in the mouth of the cave and thank God for the only relationship that is important? Perhaps we should concentrate more on our perception of the Lord as we can be assured as believers that He is always aware of us. We really need recognition from none other. We can be comfortable in how we imagine He perceives us, if we are His.

As for me, leave my photograph out of the glossy magazines and certainly off the post-office walls. Let my image only be burned into the eternal memory of God.

PUDDLE 36

MIX OR MATCH

Unfortunately, young people often get caught up in "romantic love." Whenever this discussion arises in a college class, my first question, no actually my first retort is, "How long do you think this is going to last?" Amazingly, young men seem to be more deluded than their distaff counterparts in such beliefs. Often the married, previously married, or "shacked up" women will respond, "Oh it lasts at least a couple of months." The men will adopt an authoritarian posture and declare, "Well, when I marry, it will be for life." This is where I usually have to come back and point out that the answer does not fit the question. Men actually have less of an understanding of "romantic love" than do women. The former are much more caught up in the hormonal, physical aspects of the trophy hunt. Women are still living in their pulp fiction romance books, only the horse is temporarily tethered at the hitching post.

One of the most frequent complaints I hear from women in unhappy relationships is that "I was looking for someone to depend upon, to trust, to sweep me off my feet, and I ended up marrying an adult child." Of course this is not an excuse as many women are attracted to men who are "a little bad." These fellows are exciting, someone to giggle about with girlfriends, and definitely a reclamation project. The problem is that a successful mature relationship demands a time adjustment and some of these guys still are running the roads as they enter into their mid-life crisis.

So the question that often comes up for discussion is how to attract an exciting male with a predisposition to maturity. One obvious clue is how the fellow behaves in his present time frame. If he is an idiot at age 18, he will probably be an idiot with a paunch at age 50. The serious female might also look at the family of origin. Is the paternal parent relating to the little geek or is dad remaining in his study while mother smiles and dotes over her son, who she refers to as her "little trial?" Track history also enters in. The girl must date, be courted by, and experience an extended engagement before jumping in the sack with him and definitely before taking possession. Young people roll their eyes when I suggest that a non-sexual trial period of three years is not beyond consideration.

Then there is the issue of homogeneity versus heterogeneity. Definitely the two "love birds" must both be convicted believers in the Lordship of Christ. Keeping in mind that there are a lot of goats in all religious denominations, I feel that redeemed individuals can also be found in most professing Christian faiths. It just is true that some denominations teach children in more nerve-wracking environments than others. Can you pray together? I recall one initial date when I was still unmarried which ended with the girl asking me to pray with her before I walked her to the door. My first reaction was pure panic. However, it was an honorable thing to do, I just never went back. At that point in my life she was fortunate. Young ladies, if you want to avoid awkward endings to dates with a new fellow, this will do it. However, if you can share spiritual discussions and be convinced of the other's redemption, so much the better in all ways and at all times. Just as a rabbit trail, I also dated another young lady who informed me that both her father and mother were preachers. I didn't stay around on that one too long either for obvious reasons.

In my marriage, which I consider a textbook success (I won't reveal which publisher), my wife and I are diametrically opposite in many ways. First of all, I am a man, and she is a woman. Actually that is a good starting point! She came from a liturgical church and I from a teaching church. She was a city girl and I was a farm boy. She was and remains highly social, while I like being alone with my thoughts. She was a sorority girl who taught ballet and gymnastics, while I was and am quite rigid in my concept of religious obedience. I am extremely introverted and non-verbal whereas the Wal-Mart greeters have to escort her from the store when she gets into conversations with both animate and inanimate subjects. She came from a carnivore background whereas I turned to vegetarianism when still fairly young. Strangely enough, this differentiation worked. We raised six children. Not one of them held up a bank, at least to my knowledge, and fortunately we did not end up financially supporting any one of them. Am I a romantic? Definitely, as evidenced by the aluminum dishpan that I gave to my wife on our first wedding anniversary.

So both I and my spouse have been privileged to work with young people most of our lives on an educational level. I strongly feel that God has a plan for every one of us. For some, it is to remain single and happy, (referring to Paul's admonition). For others, it may be to be married and have to struggle year after year to make the relationship work out. We have to examine our marital state and determine what we are being taught and what our purposes might be in our spiritual witness. I hope that you are not the perfect couple as then you would be boring. I hope that you are not the pinnacle of spiritual perfection, as then you would not be authentic.

I hope that you so love God and your fellow believers that they can look at your relationship and say, "You know they are kind of a weird couple, but we know to whom they belong."

PUDDLE 37

THE LIBRARY

I am fortunate to have an excellent public library in the small town in which my wife teaches school. Frequently, when I am not working and am waiting for her to complete her daily schedule, I go into the facility, to find a cubby located in a remote section of the stacks, plug in my faithful computer, and basically absorb the literary culture.

I have noticed that the regular patrons are the elderly, the lonely, and often the recent immigrant, usually from Mexico. Unfortunately, one does not see many young Anglos, especially of college-age, either at the public or the college libraries. In fact, I have found that the latter group seems to have an acquired disdain for the bound word of yesteryear and also for the boundless current news of the day. This is their loss.

Being a somewhat judgmental and opinionated individual, I have not been a fan of turning libraries into daytime flop houses for the homeless. Other public facilities are needed for this portion of our population. They do deserve access, but there has to be a discipline of purpose. Sitting around with an ill-concealed paper bag while staring at the other patrons and their little children hardly fits a need for the public. On the other hand, I have really come to appreciate the extremely elderly patrons, most of whom gingerly navigate the narrow paths between the shelves and give the impression of having achieved one additional purpose in life. They seem to read everything that they can reach from the shelves, scramble for the newspapers when they are placed out, and generally live within their own self-perception. It is wonderful that there are so many who have escaped the confines of assisted care and nursing homes, can spend their day browsing, have access to sparkling clean restrooms and more importantly preserve their self respect.

In joking with my eldest physician son recently, I opined that I preferred to avoid doctors and my choice, if God cared to hear it, would be to topple over from a chair somewhere, quietly and with dignity, and move on to be with my Lord. But realistically, looking at it, perhaps the local library would be a logical launching point. And you know, some of my elderly fellow patrons may have the same desire.

PUDDLE 38

CLOWNS AND THEIR MOTHERS

Some evenings when you are in the public arena, do you start to look for the little clown car to arrive and take some of your fellow bystanders off behind the curtains? Those are the nights when you turn to your spouse and remark, "They are really out tonight!" Last night was one of those annoying occasions. It seemed that everywhere you looked there was a "clown" and his mama. You have all seen them, so I will not bore you with too much descriptive material, just enough so that you can shake your head and think to yourself, "I've seen him or her somewhere."

The first clown was a young person. I would use the term "man" but that would be making a gross assumption. He was standing with his mama, wearing a flat driving cap. He was also sporting a puberty-entry-level goatee, a large scarf wrapped around his neck, a belly bag, and a mass of long, dirty, uncombed hair. Mama, in turn, was standing close to him, a silly little smile on her face and apparently ready to take on anyone who would ask her the natural question, "What is it?" Well, the clinician kicks in and you think, perhaps this is a case of developmental disability or perhaps his brains were fried through the use of illicit substances. He then suddenly removed his headgear, shook his head like an adolescent blond trying to impress someone, and scattered dandruff and other accumulated debris on the check-out counter. Mama continued to maintain her insane grin and

navigated her purchases though the amassed crud. I watched
closely as the pair exited the store. He resumed a rather glazed-
eyed, effeminate stroll, while mother walked as if in possession
of a trophy. The burning questions: Was there a father involved,
and does mama place her son on a wall mount at night?

Well, the evening was apparently just starting. A couple of
guys passed by, not an unusual picture in present day society.
But this image was full of stereotypes, with the more fragile of
the two working his nose like a cartoon bunny rabbit and the
stronger seeming angry and annoyed. Was this the precursor to
a tearful spat? Did wiggly have a raisin stuck up his nose and
didn't have a 2x4 available to clean it out? Were they in the store
to replace the raisins thus wasted? Was he waiting for the more
aggressive male to stop and inquire, "What is wrong, are you
going through one of your 'moods' again?" Fortunately, the duo
turned down an aisle and out of sight. Sometimes, it is best not
to do too may behavioral observations accompanied by untested
theories. Was there a mama with them? No, but I am certain that
there were two in the background...somewhere.

We then visit obnoxiousness mixed with exhibitionism.
Middle-aged mama with three high school children; two girls
definitely and one pretender. The three were blocking the
shopping aisle with some sort of gymnastic or dance routine.
They were plastered behind each other, all three with arms
raised and making an arch over their heads. Bodily coordination
was not their forte and they were slamming into canned goods
on the shelves, brushing against carts pushed by annoyed
customers and generally preparing for a pratfall. Forcing a
smile and the appearance of a gentle demeanor, I grasped the
handle of the grocery cart tightly in my hands and prepared to
accelerate into the immediate area of the unstable formation.
I mentally conjured up a small paint brush in which I would

symbolically record on the side of the buggy the number of confirmed "hits." However, as the kindness of my heart began to gush out with increased adrenaline flow, I was stopped short in my tracks. Mama with her considerable bulk was joining in the "dance." I hesitated, then reversed course, thinking that perhaps there was some sort of alien virus affecting this "ungainly" appearing foursome. Message conveyed by the older, but not wiser, shopper, "Look at me, look at me, look at my kids, aren't we hilarious?" Had I reverted to my pre-conversion behavior, a couple of cans of creamed beans would have possibly been tossed her way.

Then there is the paint mismatch, although in this case it was a bleach disaster. No, it was not a bleach spill, but almost as contaminating. My attention was drawn to two small urchins caged in a shopping cart. They looked sad, ill kept, and in my opinion possibly battered. Mama was a short, heavy set "blond" with a very dark complexion, black eyebrows, brown eyes, and not too artfully stuffed into jeans that appeared like the old time microwave popcorn bags that were just finishing popping. Hanging onto the buggy handle was something that could be loosely considered a boyfriend or the visiting uncle to the children. Mama loudly communicated emotional squeaks to anyone around her except to her children. Her facial jewelry pierced at random in her face glittered and clanged. Uncle stood and squeezed what appeared to be a facial pustule. I had just pontificated to a college class at length about the difference between nature and nurture when it is applicable to children. In this case, I could only think, "Bummer!" Mama was obviously excited, possibly anticipating the pustule extraction success on the part of her boyfriend.

You feel sad in such cases. There is undeniable predictability about the fate of these children, if they do not make the newspapers prior to maturity. You will see them in the supercenter, staring vacantly at their own children, and asking themselves, "Whose are these?"

Mamas, do you know where your children are? Do you know where you are?

PUDDLE 39

MODERN MATING

Obviously I am an old-fashioned, traditional guy, usually right in my observations, but often confused by what I see. I look at young men and think, "I wish they could have all the emotional scar tissue and experience that I have accumulated over the years at their stage of life." Would it make them better individuals? That may be open to debate. So I would just settle for being the little "angel" on their shoulder, whispering guidance and issuing warnings. By the way, such warnings may really exist, but in different forms. We do have the Holy Spirit dwelling within us, if we are among the redeemed. If we want to extend the analogy, we also have the dual force of satanic influence plus our individual fallen natures whispering in the other ear.

So, just for the entertainment and fantasy value of this discussion, let us pretend that there really is such an influencing figure on each shoulder and let's also make application to the young man just entering college without any dating experience or associations with females that circle like vultures around fresh road kill.

Most serious young men arriving on campus directly out of high school and relatively inexperienced with the opposite sex are at loose ends. They are apprehensive about the demands of the academic experience, feel awkward in making new acquaintances, and wonder what life is about to lob their way. If the student is unfortunate enough to have to live in a dormitory, it is very likely that an adjustment to a complete stranger, in a bed not more than several feet from him, has to be made. Fortunate is the student who is placed with a roommate who has the same physical cycle; that is someone who sleeps at night and works during the day. Along with dormitory living, there is the uniformly awful dining hall food. Yes, it is edible, but does one really want to eat it?

So with this stress comes the first day of class. The little angel prompts him to sit in the front of the classroom and make eye contact with the instructor. (If you do so, however, blink once in a while as it brings the teacher into his personal comfort zone.) The little adversary says to sit in the back of the room, hidden away behind a bunch of whispering girls. They are fun to watch and the instructor may not see you there. However, what happens when the self-engaged young ladies spot the isolated play-thing behind them? At best, you are drawn in as a potential antagonist against classroom etiquette and, at worst, you are being sized up as a future conquest. The little angel may counsel, "Well, you made your first mistake. Be nice but stay uninvolved until you get the lay of the land." The adversary says, "Look, she is taking you on as a challenge, you can beat her at her game, just enjoy the situation."

In the next class, the young lady most desperate moves to the seat next to you and starts a pedigree investigation. Angel says, "Discourage her and move to another seat in the next class." Devil says, "Hey big guy, you must be pretty popular, she is really coming on to you."

A couple of weeks later, you meet a charming young lady and, bringing all your courage to bare, you start a conversation. You are horrified to learn, during the brief exchange, that she has noticed that you have a girlfriend. The angel counsels, "Don't be nasty, just assure her that you have no attachments and make certain that you walk alone for a few weeks." The adversary says, "Tell her that the young lady in the classroom is just coming on to you and that you are not interested in someone who has a tattoo on her knee." Follow the adversary's advice and a nice girl would think you are a "player" and will not want to get involved.

The classroom pursuer invites you out to a party. She has already purchased a dress and assures you that your companionship is expected. The angel says, "Let her down gently, but immediately." The adversary says, "You are just being nice, she needs someone to take her to this event."

You know the rest of the story. The picture is framed and the only way out is the hurtful rejection of imagined interest. You are slandered by her friends and the other fellows laugh at your naivety.

All this description is to bring the reader to a point. It is not easy for an unattached young man to find the proper young lady for socialization and companionship on the campus. So many girls carry all sorts of baggage with them which does not necessarily have built in flares for young men who are looking, not for sexual conquest or party behavior, but for companionship and friendship. "Can't we just be friends?" doesn't always work. Therefore, this expert, in the romantic aspects of college wars, would submit the following guidelines to the young male not yet scorched by rookie mistakes or hiding in a closet in order to avoid further complications.

Things to do:

1. Be honest with any girl who shows an interest in you. Let her know that you have a priority order in life and that educational attainment is number one. Make certain that she understands that any dating you do will be strictly casual and irregular.

2. If you do date, circulate…don't tie yourself down to one "friend" and, if your college has a sorority, use care not to signal a special interest in any one of the "sisters." These women can be deadly in their competitive natures.

3. Whenever possible, limit your dating to group functions and be friendly to all the young women at such activities, even though you may be with the one that you brought. If you attend church, invite several young ladies to accompany you and choose a very early service. Why an early service?…They are usually more predictable.

4. Maintain strict adherence to reasonable hours, again to reinforce the idea that you are primarily focused on your studies.

5. Know why you are dating in the first place and maintain that focus regardless of "opportunities" or "seduction."

What not to do:

1. Do not date for sexual opportunity. That is to be reserved for marriage.

2. Do not remain uninformed as to where the young lady has been for the past several years. If she has been in college for the past fifteen years, be alert to possible intellectual limitations. If she has been living with "Fred" for the past few years and recently "broke up"don't slow down when you drop her back at her dorm.

3. Be alert to tattoos, body piercings, and black fingernails. They may be items for your lifestyle considerations.

4. Do not be a rescuer; there are pastors, psychologists, and clinical social workers for those roles.

So, after getting fully acquainted with the cultural environment, usually a year or two at a new academic institution, you meet someone who you are really attracted to physically, mentally, emotionally and, not least of all, spiritually. What then? Well, you have a decision to make. Can you make dating a special category in your life which does not interfere with your plans for educational achievement and a possible career? Some of the questions you might want to answer for yourself:

1. Does she feel the same way about you? This would be kind of helpful.
2. Is she willing to complete her education and maintain a relationship that is not sexual (from a physical standpoint) and be willing to live separately from you until some reasonable date in the future?
3. Does she share your spiritual values? Specifically, if you are a redeemed believer, is she under the Lordship of Christ also? Forget about her willingness to attend church with you. In today's society, that is hardly an indicator of belief and obedience.
4. Since there may be a wait involved, are you willing and able to handle the situation if she should change her mind about your relationship before marriage? This is important to consider, as change of mindafter marriage brings additional consequences.

While some of the guidelines are difficult in an age-group with churning hormones and anxiety about being left single, the young man, especially, must realize that marriage is not a solution but, more often, part of the problems raised in life. If you take that step, you are committed to another individual for the rest of your mortal life. Marriage must be worked at in order to be survivable. You, as the male, must take leadership and responsibility. You will find that many women are conflicted about male dominance. If this is the case, these women need to remain single. It is not shameful or a failure for a woman to remain unmarried. She will avoid all sorts of disappointment and failure. Likewise, if you are unable to "man-up" to marital responsibilities, walk the other way early on in your dating experience, and never look back.

PUDDLE 40

INTEGRITY

We all dislike phonies, people who lack authenticity in behavior. I am afraid that I am one of those individuals who is highly suspicious. My only excuse is that I have seen too much during my lifetime and carry a great deal of emotional scar tissue. It was brought to my awareness this very morning. I was preparing to leave the house when there was an insistent ring of the doorbell. Upon opening the door, I was confronted by a middle-aged gentleman carrying a yard-rake. He grinned at me, reached out to shake my hand, and then started the following well rehearsed presentation, "I know it sounds strange, but I am out of gasoline in my truck and have it parked several blocks away. I notice that your lawn needs sprucing up and I was wondering whether you would hire me to do it?" Automatically the words rolled out of my mouth, "No thank you, I appreciate the offer but I like to take care of such tasks myself." He grinned and walked off. Upon retreating back into the house, I had this twinge of remorse. Certainly I did not believe his story. Yes, I had been victimized by a lawn scheme before. No, he probably didn't even have a truck. Yes, he looked vaguely familiar, like a man who had walked off with my lawnmower without permission several years ago. However, I thought back to a friend who had without question handed a five dollar bill over to a homeless person years ago. When I challenged him on his "enabling" behavior, he rightly chastised me with the reminder that sometimes when we help others out, we are entertaining an angel unawares. Am I going to run out and find this fellow and give him some money or hire him for an unnecessary job? Absolutely not! However it does raise a question in the back of an individual's mind. Are we too cautious whom we help when they are in possible need? Isn't it all right to be "taken" once in a while when perhaps we are occasionally really helping someone out? Does this admonition refer only to "His Own" or should it reference everyone?

As Fox News intones, "We report, you decide."

PUDDLE 41

SEDUCTIVE VICTIMIZATION

Recently the news media teased and tantalized the viewers with a photo capturing a distinguished gentleman sneaking a peek at some royal cleavage. Of course, the possibility that he might have been admiring the young woman's necklace was immediately discounted.

This raises a discussion about authenticity. In this particular case, the individual's behavior was unusual in that it was some sort of "state" dinner with cameras all over the room. However, in the normal flow of life, it is understood that many women wear revealing apparel and there is a reactive curiosity of the typical male to such displays. If the potential of attracting such attention were not known to the female, she would probably dress more comfortably and modestly. In this portrayal, the lady on exhibit must have "sensed" that her table companion was allowing his gaze to wander and the result was a brief glance his way followed by a "none too subtle" tugging of a neckline which really was not especially low anyway.

There are few males who have not been subjected to what can only be categorized as "entrapment." Several years ago I was attending a liturgical church and noticed a woman walking up to the altar area to kneel to partake in communion. It was especially noteworthy that the well-endowed member of the "weaker" sex in her low cut blouse would never realize the production she would make while kneeling in front of the elderly clergyman. I thought to myself, "Surely, considering the sacredness of the rite, he will somehow avert his eyes." I could not persuade myself to avoid watching the "playing out" of the situation and was extremely disappointed and even a little offended that he "looked." However, in driving home, I attempted to cognitively sort out what I had just witnessed. Who was at fault? Was there blame to be assessed? Is the normal male so socially and spiritually disciplined that he will never notice such an obvious display? What would I have done had I been in his place? After all, hadn't I noticed when she walked down the aisle?

Over the years, working as a college instructor with certain coeds who have learned the "game" in high school and in general social situations, I have been very alert to "players." Usually during my orientation lecture, I will make reference to my clinical background and warn young people that regardless of the field of employment to which they aspire, they will have to be very alert to situations that would put them at risk for charges of sexual harassment or inappropriate behavior. This usually conveys the message that I know the rules and have no interest in such seductive gamesmanship. However, during the first few weeks of a semester, there will always be a few who will test the waters. One, from several years ago, comes to mind and is an example of manipulation on the part of a very worldly-wise young "lady." When she walked into the room, my first thought was, "I wonder how she avoids a chest cold considering the inclement weather?" A second question reared its ugly head, "I wonder how she maintains her balance?" "Did it interfere when she first learned to ride a bicycle?" Although taking a seat toward the side-rear of the classroom, I immediately became aware of her intense eye contact. Now I like eye contact from students, it shows interest and involvement, but this was a "sizing up" stare. Further questions flowed freely in my mind as I started my lecture. "Does your mother have any idea what you are wearing to class?" "Why don't colleges have hall-monitors of the same sex who enforce dress codes?" Oh yeah, that would be a violation of the freedom of expression, wouldn't it?

Other females in the class were very aware of the object of contemplation. Some glared at her, especially those who were similarly attired. The fellows, with one or two exceptions, were making gallant efforts to "not notice," while one or two were transfixed.

Then the move was made. Class was being dismissed and the little exhibitionist made a beeline to the instructor who had taken a seat behind a desk. She smiled, dropped both elbows on the desk as if to hold her head up by grasping her own ears, and inquired if her name was on the roll. Strangely, she had answered in the affirmative during the call of roll, but I guess she wanted to double check. I averted my eyes as if to watch other students walk by, but not before I noticed an extensive tattooed script on her bosom. Now I was caught in a conundrum. More unanswered questions sprung to mind. "What on earth would someone have written all over her breasts?" "Who was the tattoo operator?" "Were the words spelled correctly?" "Was proper grammar used?" "Did she have the answers to future tests in my class so affixed in advance?" "Would stretch marks blur the message?" I guess this is pondering the imponderables and I certainly will not be watching her closely to make certain that she is not cheating.

Having had six children nursed for what seemed to be a total of many years, the female breast is hardly a mystery. Having had two daughters-in-law who likewise nutritionally provided for their children in like manner, what is new under the sun? In fact, even though I am not so inclined due to spiritual obedience issues, I would probably by this time find "girly" magazines rather boring. Yes, I am a healthy male, but life experience often creates boredom. Certainly there are some males who I would consider "abnormal" who are pathologically drawn to pornography, just as there are despicable perverts who are addicted to pictures of naked children. How boring is this? In such situations, I have to chalk it off to immaturity or to an addictive personality.

It is sad that so many females buy into the "beauty myth." They are so insecure in their gender that they feel that they have to attract the male by flaunting certain physiological attributes. I would suggest that Bathsheba may have been one of those insecure types. Poor old King David fell for it hook, line, and sinker; paying a horrible price for his weakness. Young believers of the male sex are almost always warned about the "lust of the eye" and that the imagination is as deadly as the offense. So isn't there a conflict here with young men being placed at seductive risk by desperate women who have been taught that "if you have it, flaunt it"? We have to understand that there are a couple of trains of thought. One, a "God had nothing to do with it" schema, would suggest that reproduction of the species necessarily requires women to physically attract sperm donors. Therefore, the most seductive women populated the earth through their offspring while the more gentile and coy saw their genes disintegrate in the back of the cave. This does bring up a thought however, if the less attractive females did not reproduce, what was the baseline in the population at the start of time? Those who believe that "God had everything to do with it" would recognize that there has to be a physical attraction between the sexes for the continuation of the species, but ascribe to a more orderly and civil arrangement which includes responsibility, respect for the opposite sex, and order. Therefore, the framework of the family is necessary and the wandering gaze of the male, while never extinguished, is subjected to reasonable restriction. In brief, does the man ever stop noticing? No, but should he voluntarily restrict his thoughts and actions due to a greater loyalty? Definitely, yes!

Every segment of free flowing thought has to have a teaching point. In this case, "young men, recognize the 'players' and determine to morally be on top of your game. Young women, 'players' often do not win. You are desirable for who you are, what you are, and for the purpose God has given to you. Recognize this in yourself, pray and study to understand the larger picture of God's creation."

PUDDLE 42

VERBAL FLOW

On a road trip to Austin, Texas, my wife and I tried out an interesting little restaurant located just down the street from the hotel at which we were staying for a workshop. You know the type of business, well lit, some customers, and no ambulances parked strategically nearby. The atmosphere was Spartan, the food basic, but without a green tinge, and the informal atmosphere fabulous. That is except for one distraction on which perhaps only an observer of human behavior would focus. This took the form of a little girl at the next table. She must have been all of eleven years of age, cute as a bug, sitting straight in her chair, and talking. She was talking when we walked in, all during our meal, and when we walked out. Yes, she did take a breath now and then, but there was no discernible interruption in the flow of verbiage into the ether. My gaze turned to the others gathered at "her" table. There was a father, staring at his food with glassy eyes, looking like he had been working with a jackhammer all day and had sought peace and quiet in a small restaurant with his family. The mother appeared torn in attempting to pay attention to her daughter while being gracious to an older female who was probably the maternal grandmother of the "speaker." Nervous hands grasped a fork while the mother swiveled her head to focus in a pendulum rhythm on the three dinner companions. Grandmother, in turn, had a relaxed smile, was enjoying her food, and noticeably was blessed with a hearing aid which possibly had been strategically incapacitated. Some of us senior citizens become very adept survivors in such situations.

The entire scene brought to mind wonderful thoughts of my oldest granddaughter. I cannot for the life of me recall a time that she was not verbally adept. I would suspect that upon delivery she might have possibly made a comment to the delivery room nurse about the color of the swaddling blanket. She is the consummate communicator and a powerful personality. Oh well, let's be real here, she is a vivacious character.

I do not relate either authentically or in a contrived manner to infants. When I see women leaning over cribs and saying, "Oh it is so beautiful," I am thinking that Pinocchio's nose has just grown another inch. Babies have to have personalities, not merely lay there, soil diapers, drool sour milk, and make demanding screams. Well, this little damsel (my granddaughter) met her grandfather's expectations early on. Some relationships are supportive and affectionate. She had plenty of this from loving parents and two older brothers who remarkably survived the new "apple of the family's eye." My relationship with her was conflicted from the start. From the beginning, it was a test of wills and of mutual provocation. Children have to earn and deserve attention, not merely wallow around and have it cascade upon them.

The contest commenced early on. One evening while regally seated in a car seat and holding on to her "security" blanket, my wife reached through the window and said something infantile like, "Nice blankie." Don't you hate it when grown adults use baby talk? To make certain that the child was confronted with the reality of life, I then approached her and when she pre-offered the sodden piece of cloth, I took it and said firmly, "My blankie" and walked away. A torrent of sound emitted from the car, not of sorrow upon losing a treasure, but more of pure feminine rage. My wife made me give it back, somewhat to my disgust. Following this social interchange, my granddaughter stiffened, no actually became rigid, for sometime whenever I made an appearance. Her mother, being a fine Christian woman, worked valiantly with the child to teach her all about teasing. Little did she know that I had been dead serious. A new plateau was reached and after a couple of years the child walked up to me when I had arrived at her house (notice with a little daughter it is she who is in possession) and offered me a wild flower that she had plucked from the yard. I am certain that mother had directed this rapprochement and, after a lot of urging, the obedient child took the gracious step. She handed the beautiful hand-gathered gift to me, I thanked her, and then watching her intently, put the flower into my mouth and ate it. A look of horror crossed the child's face. She covered her own mouth with her hands and ran to the safety of my wife. I couldn't quite understand the reaction as incorporation of a gift is the finest compliment one can give. My daughter-in-law was less gracious in making an observation that she hoped the flower had been picked where the dogs ran. I don't really understand the implication, but there must have been something negative there.

Now, however, we have reached another stage in our coexistence. She will take my hand, although she always twists it. She will talk to me, but usually with her back turned. She will share items, but never allow them to leave her hand.

This is what I call character development.

I submit these "tongue in cheek" observations to grandfathers everywhere. Relate on a positive basis early with your granddaughters. Make certain that they know that they can trust you and predict your behaviors. Learn to appear to be listening to their constant chatter and especially do not allow them to observe your pain. Such little ladies make up the future of America.

PUDDLE 43

THE COMPASS

Sometimes we fall into a state of awareness that might be labeled "intersection theory." It seems as if everything piles up on you and you find yourself drowning in oblivion, trying to break to the surface and desperately gasp the cool air of stability and security.

I had a weekend such as this recently. It started out innocently enough. I decided to forego my usual regimen of steel cut oatmeal and homemade raisin toast early Saturday morning as my wife had a desire for a good scrambled egg. Why she had never achieved the ability to master such a pedestrian food item is a mystery. Perhaps it is the memory of too many frying pans that were neglected while egg residue solidified in them. Anyway, simple enough request. We had not been overly impressed with some of the chain type food establishments, so knowing of two older mom and pop eateries, we set off across town. Much to our surprise, the first establishment had a large "For Sale" sign in the window. This business was located away from the main thoroughfares and in the past had served the fine residents of an older neighborhood. Well, such is the outcome of change. We drove across the city to another similar restaurant and this time the sign was a little more positive, "Open at 11." Reversing course, we returned to the apartment and the oats were placed on the range. Kind of strange when progress standardizes restaurant food to the point that personalization and individualization disappear.

Anyway, later in the day we had been invited to a viewing of *Atlas Shrugged-Part 1,* at the University with some believing friends. It was sponsored by a student group, but noticeably the majority of those attending were gray-haired and gave that distinct impression of being retired from the workforce. There was a powerful message conveyed by the film, subject to individual interpretation by the discerning viewer. I was left with a sense of increased awareness and a strange sense of dread, mitigated by the companionship of those of like-mind.

Sunday morning found me flicking through the blessings of extended cable access television searching for a particular religious program that I usually watch while consuming another bowl of steel cut oats. For some reason I had difficulty locating the correct channel and this merged with my sensitized awareness from the previous day. I became disheartened by what I realized to be the regular viewing fare of many people. The programming was debased, pagan, anti-Christian and mentally deconstructive. I finally found the program that I had been seeking, but the feeling of alienation from the humanistic portion of society was overwhelming.

In the afternoon, we made our trip to one of the local nursing homes, with individual packages of donuts (yes, I know, not nutritionally correct, but have you ever tried to transport cooling steel cut oats?) One lady, in particular, took a piece of coarse sandpaper to my already prickly awareness. She sat in her wheelchair and talked about the plan for the end of her life. She realized that there would be no returning to a home and family. She would live out the rest of her years in some sort of institutional setting. Then came the big whap, "You know when I was younger, I had a relative that had to live in a nursing home.

I think I am here because this is God's punishment for not being more of a friend to her." Immediate thoughts of false assurance leap to one's mind. Fortunately, before I could say anything superficial, I heard my wife assure her that God has a purpose in everything that happens to a believer. She pointed out to this wonderful lady how she was always ministering to others in any way possible, whether it be holding the hand of a dying fellow resident or wheeling over with a cup of coffee for someone who could not move around as well as she could.

Monday morning, we were on the move again. I was driving my wife to her school and I was going to spend some time working on this manuscript and then I intended to do some work on my mother's lawn. During the thirty minute trip, we always listen to a specific radio broadcast on Christian Radio. The speaker was talking about the focus of believers when it comes to our present deteriorating political climate. His overriding point was that we must be obedient to the rulers that God has appointed over us and that our primary concern should be on getting the message of salvation out to everyone possible. An overriding point: both an unbelieving preacher and an unbelieving criminal will end up in the same place, the abode of those separated from God. As believers, we must spread the Word to both.

With the foregoing observations in mind, can anyone not understand how isolated the believer feels in our present age? Certainly there are many who are much more sophisticated and learned than this writer. Likewise, almost any of the redeemed are more deserving of God's love and grace than this writer. However, through grace alone, through the perfect sacrifice of Christ, and claiming His righteousness in place of my sinful nature, I am one of those who believe, and I feel isolated. Why does there seem to be such a small covey of the redeemed walking the earth right now? Getting back to the task at hand, how do I turn this segment into a "puddle" which will meet the criteria of a knowing chuckle?

First of all, we must rejoice that we are not alone. Certainly I have a believing wife and several friends about whose passport to Heaven I have no concern. There are others around us who have demonstrated the fruit of the Spirit that could only be enabled by God's grace. Remember, everything that we have and are comes from above. The Holy Spirit and demons cannot coexist in the Holy Temple of God, which each believer is. God has allowed two groups of people to exist, those who are His and those who are not. Believers do not deliberately continue in disobedience while unbelievers do live in rebellion to God. Sometimes it is difficult to recognize your brothers and sisters in Christ because of all the muck and confusion produced by the popular entertainment and corruption that surround us. Believers are around us, perhaps their Godly behaviors are not blatant or "in your face," but look for them. I found one couple in the workplace, slowly recognizing their allegiance through behaviors rather than words. My wife and I found another couple whom we had known in a church relationship for many years, but it was only within the last few years that God identified them to us as the fellow redeemed. Sometimes the organizational church confuses the ease of identification as there are so many who would be called "Christians" who are not "Believers."

Does this mean that we cannot laugh and enjoy each other? Do we have to be stilted and so "good" in our behavior that we are boring? Absolutely not! I have found fellow believers to be "fun" to be around, relaxed in that they do not have to "play-act" because they are with people who think and understand like they do. We can be assured that God is constantly aware of all our thoughts, even our failings, and still loves us. This love is not because we are so special, but because we are chosen of

Him, are His possessions, and are already with Him now and will continue to be with Him for eternity.

So whether we are standing in the middle of DFW airport with myriads of harried people milling around or whether we are sitting alone by a lake side with only the mosquitoes as our companions, we are closer than a word away from our God because we are actually only a thought away.

This is merely a temporary stop along the way. Some suggest that God is using this as a period of character development. I think it is more of a demonstration project, showing those who are evil that God, who is good, has a plan for those He has redeemed and nothing can destroy this final resolution.

So laugh with those who are His. Rejoice in the ever-presence of God. Marvel at His grace and handiwork. Talk up the gift that He has given to those who He loves. Life does not have to make rational sense. We should not spend extraordinary time in wondering why God allows so much evil and distortion around us. Everything has a purpose, a plan, and an unalterable outcome. Rejoice, always, rejoice.

PUDDLE 44

A DAUGHTER WHO ALSO HAPPENED TO BE BLOND

It was a pleasure to have a daughter whose sense of humor and reactive timing to the unusual were on par with the best. However, this daughter was also susceptible to the careful planning of her father, which often resulted in peals of laughter from her siblings as she fell prey to various and assorted pranks.

Knowing that she received regular telephone calls from various amorous, pubescent boys each evening and taking into consideration that all six of the siblings would race to answer the telephone, the setting was natural. You take one part of sibling competition, mix with an aggressive nature, and sprinkle with a narcissistic need to receive such attention; the table was set.

Mustard was carefully applied to the earpiece of the old brown telephone, just out of sight of the lunging responder. Long blond hair would not be drawn back while the left hand was used to fend off her family competition for communication opportunities. The headset would slap against the right ear, followed by a howl of disgust. What made the joke really funny is that my daughter, the blond, would make the same mistake time after time, when the application of the condiment was spaced out by a few days.

She was a heartbreaker for the little hopeful initiates who would be treated like royalty on the phone, but who usually were not considered for a date. It was so devastating to the young men that I carefully cut paper tombstones out of construction paper and lined them up above a living room door with each young man's name on it when the object of his desire shook her blond tresses and rejected his advances.

She was also a "gamer" of the highest order. I would drive her to school in my old, beat up truck, knowing that she preferred to be left out toward the rear of the parking lot, partly because of me, but probably, even more so, because the pickup was not a seemly carriage for a proper young lady. One morning, a girlfriend of hers asked to catch a ride to school with us. My blond carefully slid over the protruding wire springs of the seat while her friend pulled the passenger door closed with authority. She was stylishly dressed, was carrying her clarinet, and reflected disdain for the need to be transported in such a lowly vehicle. This time, instead of stopping at the rear of the lot, we meandered to the front of the school where various and sundry middle-school students loitered awaiting the morning bell. The little girl politely thanked me for the "lift" and reached for the door handle. I stopped her in an apologetic tone and informed her that the door was broken and would not release from the inside. My daughter's eyes sparkled. In her discomfort, the friend did not stop to think that I could step out of the driver's side and allow her to slide through or that I could walk around to open the door from the outside. I cautioned her to be careful as she squirmed through the door window making exit from our presence. My blond daughter then handed the band instrument through the window to the thoroughly embarrassed young lady, being watched by her scholastic acquaintances. Then came the piece de resistance. My daughter scooted over and opened the door from the inside. The story lived on for years, whenever we sought a good laugh.

Less humorous was the mistake my wife and I made in purchasing a young Chow puppy for the blond. For those of you who know the personality characteristics of such a breed, you are asking yourself right now, were these people insane? We were unaware of what we were getting, seeing instead a beautiful bundle of fur, wrapped up in a blanket by the blond and transported home on her lap. The dog bonded with her, sleeping outside of her sliding glass door when she was gone and guarding her room from within at night. I always wondered if the imprint factor was involved and that the dog saw my blond before he recognized his mother. She was loved with a fanatic affection by that dog, while the rest of us nursed our nips and avoided contact with him as much as possible. I decided one day while she was in school that it would be interesting to get this dog accustomed to riding in a vehicle. So I loaded him up in the old truck and drove to a nearby shopping center. Stopping the truck, the dog bounded over my lap out the door. The chase was on. He remained approximately one block ahead of me while I chased after him, praying the he would not take a chunk out of some little old lady who just happened to get in his way. Finally I gave up and walked back to the truck, having decided to call the animal control folks and encouraging them to shoot him on sight. I opened the door, lifted a leg to the running board, and a golden flash with a black tongue bounded onto the passenger side seat. The fun must have been in the chase and he didn't want to be left alone downtown.

He and I had a strange relationship. He would come running at me when I returned home from work, would set his teeth on my arm, but would never bite down. I suppose that in a sense I was his walking dental floss.

Just another blond with whom to contend!

PUDDLE 45

PROVOCATEURS

Don't you get tired of people who seem to go out of their way to bring out the worst in you? It almost seems that some people were placed here to do nothing more than to poke and prod others until the latter finally lose their cool.

I was talking to some folks recently about some of the employers who want to reduce their payrolls by accepting the early resignations of their older, long-term employees. They cannot be up front and honest due to the civil protections employees have nowadays, so they find all sorts of disguised techniques to reach their goal. Perhaps it is something dramatic such as a change in duties with the employer knowing that the targeted employee could not succeed under the new requirements. Perhaps it is moving the person into an office that resembles a closet because of a "needed" reorganization. It could even be something so insignificant as the disappearance of an Ethernet cable or the removal of WI-FI accessibility. All is done to provoke.

A few years ago I was parked in front of a market in Dallas, only to have a car pull up beside me and the driver harangue me about being parked in a handicapped space. Being uncertain as to my guilt, I apologized and starting backing out of the space, only to discover that it was not so marked. The antagonized driver realized his mistake at the same time. I pulled back in while he stared straight ahead. I did not say a word knowing that my presence was making him uncomfortable enough. Certainly I was provoked, but it was hardly worth letting him see that he had gotten to me.

I turn on some of the cable commentaries and listen to biased and downright distorted versions of obvious facts. Yes, I could turn them off, but I like to watch patterns, and there are plenty available for analysis. Why do they do such deceitful things? Certainly not to provoke me, but there are a group of people who begin to believe their own prevarications.

If you really want to be exposed to provocation, go to your neighborhood salad bar and watch people serve themselves. It can become real ugly. Watch people line up for a sale on the so-called "Black Friday." On second thought, do not watch them.

You ever notice how difficult it is to "like" or love your fellow human beings? Are they all weird? Are you and I the only ones who are normal? From a clinical viewpoint, one might theorize that they are all "insecure." Perhaps they were all raised in an addicted family with a pedophile uncle living in the side room.

You certainly could make your own list of provocateurs. There is the fellow who spits yellow substances on the sidewalk that you tread and the perfectly healthy woman of great girth who mounts the little shopping scooter and angle parks in the aisle. Thinking of which, several years ago, I watched such a "lady" make herself really obnoxious and actually endanger other shoppers in her rudeness. I decided to take a little time and watch to determine how she transferred from the electric cart to her vehicle. When she finally checked out and, by the way, the checker had to carry the purchases to her as she would not remove herself from the seat, she proceeded to the entrance and parked the "panting" cart. She reached into a large bag that she carried, took out a pair of fancy high-heeled shoes, placed them on and walked nicely to her car, carrying her purchases. One could go on and on…and on…and on.

However, did you ever think of how much we must provoke God with our behaviors? We act like we are smarter than He is. We really do not need Him unless we are in a bind. He is there to serve our needs and to be available if we ever have to dial His number. His professional earthly liaisons are often as worldly as the rest of us. We entertain ourselves with psychological, management, and entertainment games and call it worship. We think it right to attend His House clad in our casual rags while we entertain friends in formal attire.

So if God can tolerate all the ways in which I provoke him in immature, thoughtless, selfish ways; I guess I will have to learn to tolerate the behaviors of my fellow brothers and sisters and even those who do not know Him.

PUDDLE 46

NEVER LET THEM SEE YOU SWEAT

It is interesting to watch people casually shake hands, whether it is a form of greeting, saying good-bye, or an indication of some sort of agreement. It often appears that the dominant personality engaged in the handshake is the last to release his/her grip. In fact, good old "Type A" will usually get in a casual "body-touch" on the victim of lesser self-confidence to reinforce the concept of who the "Alpha Dog" in the yard might be.

However, it may be a mistake to share this observation with close friends in casual social situations. We, as indicated elsewhere, are breakfast people. There is nothing quite like a quiet meal in a friend's kitchen, with hot coffee, great scrambled eggs, and even better companionship. One morning, prior to sitting down at the table, I shared my observations as to who releases a handshake first. The couple that we were visiting are traditional Christians of the first order and, as such, they offer up thanksgiving to God prior to partaking of the food about to be consumed while joining hands with their guests. So, you mix a "people watcher's" observation, with hand-holding, and a woman of strong determination, and you end up with two people unwilling to release first. Being a gentleman, I had to "cave" but the next time I will have to make certain that I sit between my wife and the host-husband so that I do not have to prove my point. If I do again sit next to her, I quite possibly will be typing my next manuscript using only my left hand.

EPILOGUE

It is my hope that your "puddles" overflow as you add your own thoughts to this observational commentary on life. While I have attempted to remain "light" in my observations, I realize that we are in serious times. Many born after World War II are only beginning to experience some of the sacrifices endured by their grandfathers and grandmothers that were needed to support their families, to maintain their traditional values, and to ensure a future for their children.

We must learn to recognize the blessings that we have been given by God, to this generation and to this nation. We must also recognize that there is a requirement of obedience, to love Him above all things and our neighbors as ourselves through the working of the Holy Spirit within each believer. It is plain that those He loves, He also chastises. It is also without doubt that those who reject Him will in turn be rejected.

So therefore; study, pray, obey, and prepare. No one is certain how or when temporal time for them will end. Remain faithful, find solace in the company of fellow believers, do not compromise or fall into doubt, and do not lose your grip on trust and hope in God, our Creator and Savior.

In the meantime, appreciate those around you, extend your love to them, and learn to find humor in the most common of your observations.ADV/SSV

Would you like to see your manuscript become a book?

If you are interested in becoming a PublishAmerica author, please submit your manuscript for possible publication to us at:

mybook@publishamerica.com

You may also mail in your manuscript to:

**PublishAmerica
PO Box 151
Frederick, MD 21705**

www.publishamerica.com

CPSIA information can be obtained at www.ICGtesting.com
Printed in the USA
BVOW05s1256051214

378129BV00001B/107/P